A STUDIO BOOK

ANDREAS FEININGER

TREES

TREES

THE VIKING PRESS · NEW YORK

To Wysse—
Who sparked this book and stayed with it all the way

Published in 1968 by The Viking Press,
625 Madison Avenue, New York, New York 10022

Distributed in Canada by Penguin Books Canada Limited

Third printing April 1978

LIBRARY OF CONGRESS CATALOGING IN PUBLICATION DATA
Feininger, Andreas, 1906–
    Trees.
    (A Studio book)
    Includes index.
    1. Trees. 2. Trees—Pictorial works. I. Title.
QK475.F4 1978   582'.16   78-2382
ISBN 0-670-72943-4

Printed in the United States of America

Acknowledgment is made to Time Inc. for permission to
reproduce the following plates: 1, 14, 117, 118,
120, 122, 142, and 144. Copyright © Time Inc.

CONTENTS

Acknowledgments

I wish to express my great indebtedness to the following individuals, corporations, and agencies which, by supplying invaluable and authoritative information, and permitting me to use material prepared by them, have helped make this book richer, more accurate, more effective, and more complete than it would have been without their valuable contributions:

Dr. Howard Irwin of The New York Botanical Garden, who read and checked for scientific accuracy the botanical part of the text.

U.S. Department of Agriculture, Soil Conservation Service, Educational Relations Service, Mr. Walter E. Jeske, Head.

U.S. Department of Agriculture, Forest Service, Division of Forest Economics and Marketing Research, Mr. H. R. Josephson, Director.

Mr. Hal McElroy, District Ranger, Inyo National Forest, Bishop, Calif.

The University of Arizona, Laboratory of Tree-Ring Research, Dr. Bryant Bannister, Director, and Dr. C. W. Ferguson, Assistant Professor of Dendrochronology.

American Forest Products Industries, Inc., Washington, D. C.

The American Forestry Association, Washington, D.C.

Georgia-Pacific Corporation, Portland, Oregon.

Weyerhaeuser Company, Tacoma, Washington.

Introduction

I am sitting in the shade of a dogwood tree at the edge of a wood overlooking a lake. As the sun's heat penetrates the cool of morning, the air buzzes with insect stridulations, a swallowtail flashes its sunshine wings, a hornet alights on the arm rest of my weather-beaten folding chair and begins to rasp off tiny flakes of wood for its nest. I am the center of a world of blue and green—the blue of water and sky, the green of hemlock and birch, hornbeam and maple, hickory, ash, and oak. My seat is an island in a sea of leaves—and what better place for collecting my thoughts in order to write a book on trees?

I had returned only recently from a strenuous but enormously stimulating journey devoted entirely to studying and photographing trees. With my wife Wysse I had driven eleven thousand miles in twelve weeks across the length and breadth of the United States, to see once more the magnificent trees that are distinctive to our country—the Northern hardwood forests, the palms and live oaks of the South, and above all, the giant sequoias, towering redwoods, and ancient bristlecone pines of the West—setting out on what still may prove an impossible task: to capture on film and sensitized paper, in color and in black and white, and eventually in published pictures and words, something of the thought-provoking grandeur of trees. For I had set my mind on making a new kind of tree book—a project that had kept me occupied on and off for the previous nine years—not a textbook or manual, nor a tree-identification book, nor still another picture book proving that trees are beautiful, but a tree-appreciation book.

It seems to me there is a need for just this kind of book. In our largely urban society, the ability to appreciate trees has become dulled—the ability to see the wonder in a tree, the magic and the mystery, the indiscribable peace and contentment that can fill our hearts when we walk the wild woods. Nowadays, too many people consider trees nothing more than a cash crop—so many board feet of lumber, so many dollars per acre of pulp. If a tree can be sold, or if it is in the way of "progress," the practice is to cut it down without a second thought, no matter how stately and beautiful it is or how many generations must pass before another will grow in its place. In a small town near my home in Connecticut, most of the shade trees that once were the pride of the village have been felled to make space for gas stations and supermarkets. Now, the hot sun beats down relentlessly on acres of blacktop and cement where people used to stroll in the cool green shade of trees.

Such thoughtless destruction of trees goes on all over the world, and all of us are losers. But what we have lost are intangible qualities that cannot be expressed in dollars and cents. How does one price the soaring rise of a century-old tree, the protective spread of its crown, the restful shade it provides on sweltering summer days? I created this book in the hope of making more people aware of the intangible values that trees can give—values to lift the spirit and refresh the soul of man.

New Milford, Connecticut   *Andreas Feininger*

I
The Importance of Trees

Man's life, his origin, his uniqueness, and perhaps even the continuation of his very existence, are inextricably tied to the life of trees. Had there been no trees, it seems more than likely that the human race would never have come into being; should the trees die, it is not inconceivable that man too would become extinct.

These are sweeping statements. But the findings of prehistory, history, and science—and in particular paleontology, archeology, anthropology, comparative anatomy, and ecology—by now add up to such an impressive body of supporting evidence that these statements can no longer be doubted. This evidence will be presented later. But the conclusions may be cited right here where our story begins: we must protect the trees or face disastrous consequences.

At the dawn of humanity, perhaps a million years ago, the forest was home to the small bands of the emerging race of dawnmen. Fossil evidence in conjunction with comparative anatomy seems to show that man got his start in the forest.

In prehistoric times, trees were worshiped as gods. They were sometimes considered embodiments of the dark and fearful powers of nature, of lightning and thunder and storm—incarnations of spirits and demons that had to be propitiated with sacrifices and chants, just as they are still propitiated by some primitive tribes.

Then came a period when, as ancient legends and surviving written records show, trees were revered as dwelling places of divine beings, both vengeful and benign. If pacified by flattery and adoration, these tree divinities would grant fertility to man and beast, abundance at harvest time, and success in commerce and war.

This belief gave way with the rise of Christianity. According to Christian dogma, man was created in the image of God, and the world was his to subjugate and use. Tree worship became equivalent to heresy.

And as man's reverence for trees diminished while his numbers increased, trees were more and more viewed as a commodity—a seemingly inexhaustible supply of wood for lumber and fuel, buildings and ships, farm implements, tools, and the necessities of daily life. This attitude worked well as long as the number of people was relatively small, but it became increasingly dangerous as populations and consequent wood consumption grew.

The turning point in the United States came during the first half of this century when two facts became obvious: the "inexhaustible" supply of trees was dwindling so rapidly that, if the steadily accelerating rate of cutting were permitted to go on, the forests would be exhausted within a foreseeable, uncomfortably short time; and the wholesale cutting of trees made the denuded land disastrously vulnerable to the onslaught of the elements. Floods and storms tore away the soil, watersheds began to fail, and rampant erosion brought the specter of total ruin to large areas of the country.

Realizing this danger, a handful of far-sighted men and women began a campaign of enlightenment which gradually aroused the public's interest, forced government agencies to act and legislatures to pass protective laws that set aside large tracts of still unspoiled land as recreational areas and national parks, and more or less succeeded in changing people's attitude toward trees from one of disinterested ignorance to one of modest concern. Today even the big lumber companies, which only a few decades ago were the worst despoilers of the forests, are largely conservation-conscious—not because their policy-makers had a change of heart, but because they finally came to realize that, in order to continue in business, they must plant at least as many trees as they cut.

Today, the future of the trees seems reasonably assured, although the pressure of our constantly increasing population creates new dangers which I'll discuss later. But at least the general public's attitude toward trees has improved. Signs of this can be found on both the smallest and the largest scale. When a community's beautiful old trees are in danger of being sacrificed to "progress"—the widening of a street, the creation of a new housing development—public voices are raised in protest: a woman's garden club objects, the local chapter of the Audubon Society draws up a resolution, community leaders circulate a petition. And our legislators, in spite of continuous heavy pressure by vested interest—ranchers and cattlemen, mining, oil, and lumber companies—are becoming increasingly conservation-minded, with the result that federal lands are better protected against misuse, wilderness areas are being set aside as inviolable, and new refuges added to those already existing.

But let's not rejoice too soon. This is the kind of fight that must be fought constantly. Unless we wild-tree preservationists remain alert, the forces of selfishness and greed may still get their way and the big and beautiful commercially desirable trees such as redwood and sequoia, mahogany and walnut, the ancient oaks, and a host of others will disappear from our woods. The wilderness will be invaded, "subjugated," and "developed," and in the end our forests will consist of endless rows of carefully nurtured domesticated trees planted and harvested like wheat.

Trees are an integral part of nature, and, as the relatively new science of ecology—the study of interrelationships between living organisms and their environment—has shown, no part of nature can be tampered with without affecting all other parts. In this respect, nature is like a delicately adjusted machine: fool around with one of its components and you disturb the proper working order of the rest.

Unfortunately, however, many people still don't care what happens "in nature." The following summary is intended to show how anything that happens on a large scale to trees also affects our own human interests. As far as man is concerned, trees are important in three respects: economically, ecologically, and spiritually.

The economic role of trees

On Sunday, December 3, 1961, *The New York Times* published a record edition in terms of bulk. Each issue contained 678 pages and weighed 6 pounds 3½ ounces. The press run was 1,458,558 copies. Printing this staggering pile required 4,550 tons of paper, and newsprint, as everyone knows, is made from wood pulp. Manufacturing the pulp for this single edition required the wood from over 77,000 full-grown trees! The average age of these trees was seventy years, and cutting them left a 360-acre hole in the forest. It took all this to publish a single edition of a single newspaper in a single city, read in the morning and thrown away in the afternoon.

Paper is only one of the innumerable necessities of modern life that derive from the forest, although it is one of the most important in terms of value and bulk. Others are timber, lumber, and plywood; turpentine and creosote; maple sugar and Christmas trees and the thousands of finished products made of wood without which contemporary civilization is unthinkable—wooden furniture; magazines and books; rayon fabrics and photographic film; containers, packing and wrapping material; toilet paper and facial tissues; wood for the fireplace and charcoal for the grill; ice-cream sticks, toothpicks, matches, ad infinitum.

The forest products industry ranks as the fourth largest in the United States. In 1963, 1,452,000 full-time employees drew a payroll of over 7 billion dollars and produced goods valued at 29 billion 356 million dollars. The story of America's forests, beginning with the colonists clearing spaces for farms and towns, through the robber barons' "cut and get out" exploitation, to modern concepts of conservation through sustained-yield forestry, is a long and painful one. It begins on December 12, 1620, when the Pilgrims left the Mayflower to take possession of a virgin continent. Survival in those early days depended on subjugating the forest, which blanketed land urgently needed for crops. The forest had to be destroyed by ax and fire before a family could stake out a farm. It provided logs and timbers to build blockhouses and cabins strong enough to withstand attacks by Indians and warm enough to resist the bitter winter cold; it supplied wood for cooking and heat, and yielded game for the table. The forests seemed endless, the wood supply unlimited, and the number of settlers was small; so the Pilgrims had no concern about using the forests as they pleased. It was this understandable viewpoint of the colonists which shaped the attitude of future generations—an attitude that later was to do irreparable harm.

Not surprisingly, the forest industry was America's first business. Even before the Pilgrims stepped ashore in Massachusetts, English bankers and traders had imported timber and other forest products from the New World. The oldest surviving record of this trade tells of a shipload of sassafras bark gathered along the coasts of Maine and Massachusetts in 1603 by one Martin Pring. In 1608 the first shipload of the Virginia Company left for England with a cargo of forest products: tar, pitch, and turpentine, essential materials for shipbuilding and repair; potash, a necessary ingredient of soap obtained by burning wood; lumber and manufactured wood products such as clapboard and wainscoting for houses.

While the colonists were settling the New World, the great naval powers, England, Holland, France, and Spain, were fighting endless battles at sea. Ship losses were heavy, and the demand for replacement exceeded the available timber supply, particularly of oak, needed to timber hulls and keels, and pine, used for masts and spars. So it was only natural that Britain looked to its colony in America for materials it no longer could get from its own depleted forest, especially the great boles of white pine, which in size surpassed anything that Europe could produce, for mast wood. Lumbering became a thriving business along the entire Eastern coast of North America, and the first sawmill was erected around 1623 at York in Maine. It never stopped operating until the virgin timber of the region was completely gone.

Ruthless exploitation of the new country's timberlands soon brought on a shortage of easily accessible big pines, and the first conservation laws were passed. To no avail—they were ignored, and the forest receded under the onslaught of fire and ax as the lumbermen drove westward, crossing the boundaries of the land grants and invading the "Crown Lands," or royal domain, in their search for the big trees which were the foundation of a thriving trade in ship masts, not only to England but also to its enemies Spain and Portugal and ultimately to places as far away as Africa and Madagascar.

Trouble began under the reign of William and Mary when those monarchs decreed the largest specimens of white pine the property of the Royal Navy. Not surprisingly, this decree enraged the Americans who had risked their lives cutting these big trees in forests infested with hostile Indians and floating the enormous timbers down the wild rivers to civilization. Cutting trees marked by the King's Broad Arrow came to be considered almost a patriotic deed, even if

it had to be done under cover of darkness or by loggers disguised as Indians to foil the spy system set up by the British, which provided that the denounced offender be flogged and the accusing spy be given the offender's land. When at last revolution swept the country, Congress in 1774 stopped all export to Britain, effectively cutting off its mast supply and forcing the British navy to fight with inferior masts of jointed heavy Riga fir.

The winning of independence was followed by a century of growth and expansion unparalleled by any country in history. Timber was the new country's greatest source of wealth, and its people lost no time in exploiting the forests to the limit. A new type of hero was born, the American lumberjack, the greatest woodsman of all time. His feats of courage, hardiness, and strength became the theme of countless folk songs and found ultimate expression in the legendary figure of Paul Bunyan. Accompanied by Babe, his blue ox, Paul Bunyan performed deeds of derring-do on a titanic scale, deeds which still live in the tales told around the campfires in the great North woods. He was the strongest man who ever lived. When his Swedish foreman, big Hels Helsen, challenged him to a fight, they fought all over the Dakotas, rolling and kicking so much that they knocked down all the trees. When the fight ended, nothing was left of the mountains but some blood-soaked lumps of clay which are now the Black Hills. When whisky-trees were still growing in Kansas, Paul let Babe loose to chew off the trees so that his men would work instead of getting drunk—and ever since Kansas has been dry. When the big spring rains came up from China and it rained forty days and nights upward through the ground, all the wild Western logging country together with Paul Bunyan and his blue ox disappeared forever in the flood.

But American logging history was not all epic and picturesqueness. Behind the heroic deeds immortalized in legend and song lurks a story of bribery and perjury, waste and exploitation, corruption and greed. This is what happened:

Independence won, seven of the original states laid claim to some 230 million acres of virgin territory to the west. Between 1781 and 1802, the states ceded these areas to the newly formed federal government, which thus became the owner of large tracts of land. This was the beginning of the system of public domain, in which certain land was owned outright by the federal government and was not merely territory open to all comers.

As the nation expanded westward, most of the newly opened land became part of the public domain. After the Texas, Mexico, Louisiana, and Alaska Purchases, the public domain consisted of 1 billion 807 million acres. Subsequent acquisition of land from private owners brought the federally owned lands to an all-time high of 1 billion 855 million acres.

The thought behind the acquisition of these enormous tracts of land by the government was to ensure its orderly development as it was sold piece by piece to settlers. Under the Land Ordinance of 1785, the first tracts of public domain land were sold in lots of 36 square miles at a price of one dollar per acre, but soon a new system of land partition was introduced by a committee of the Continental Congress, under the chairmanship of Thomas Jefferson, which divided land checkerboard-fashion in one-mile squares called "sections," each section containing 640 acres. A settler could buy as little as a quarter section.

Although at first the government had no objection to selling large tracts of land to a single buyer, this policy was later reversed and by 1834 the minimum that could be bought had been lowered to 40 acres. The new policy was designed both to encourage the thrifty small settler who would hold on to his land, make it self-supporting, and increase its taxability, and also to prevent the formation of large monopolistic enterprises. Unfortunately, the latter was precisely what the lumber industry required, for it was impossible to erect a sawmill and operate it at a profit on the limited amount of land that a single purchaser could legally buy from the government.

To get around these restrictions, the lumber operators used every dishonest trick they could devise. For example, under the Timber and Stone Act of 1878, any citizen could buy up to 160 acres of nonagricultural land for $2.50 an acre without being required to live on it, provided he swore that the land was for his own personal use. This proved to be a godsend to the lumber operators. Their tree scouts, after locating a desirable tract of timberland, would round up a number of drifters in the nearest town and take them out into the woods on a holiday. There are even reports of trainloads being brought out by chartered train. Out among the big trees, each bum was led to a

specific section which he staked in accordance with instructions received. Afterwards, the group was taken to the local branch of the Land Office where each filed his claim under the Timber and Stone Act, swearing that he was buying the land for his own personal use. Then he would pay the fee with money given him by the tree scout, leave, and immediately put his land to personal use by selling his claim to the scout for fifty dollars.

Acquisition of timberland by lumber companies through fraudulent claims became commonplace. The whole grim story of crookedness and corruption is eloquently told in *The Great Forest* by Richard G. Lillard. One saga tells of a man who "conducted water upon the land" as required by the law to perfect his title to a tract of "desert" (which just happened to carry a fine stand of timber). What the man had done was load his wagon with a plow, a barrel of water, and a bunch of "witnesses" and drive one morning to his claim. There he unloaded his plow and scratched a furrow on a dry hillside, knocked the bung out of his barrel, and let the water run down into his "ditch" while his witnesses stood by witnessing. Then he went back and filed his claim, his conscience at ease because he had complied with the letter of the law.

Another man became the owner of valuable timberland by crossing it in a boat. Checking a suspicious title, a federal agent found that a tract of land which the document led one to believe was marshy and wet actually was quite dry. Marshy land being not very desirable and therefore relatively easy to come by, a tree locator had acquired title to the tract by swearing that he had crossed it in a boat. What he did not reveal was that his boat had been mounted on wheels and pulled by a yoke of oxen.

If it proved impossible to acquire legal title to timber —no matter how fraudulent the means—the next best way was to steal it from public lands. In time, this poaching on government property took on such huge proportions that it could no longer be ignored even in faraway Washington, and in 1853, a representative of the Land Office named Isaac Willard was sent to Michigan to put a stop to timber poaching. He actually succeeded in confiscating a quantity of lumber stolen from government land, but when he tried to sell it at auction, the hostile public refused to bid and instead nearly lynched him, killing one of his deputies during the brawl. Willard requested help, and the gunboat *Michigan* was sent to Manistee, the town on the eastern shore of Lake Michigan which had been the scene of the fracas. Sailors landed and at bayonet point arrested many rioters, some of whom were later convicted and fined.

Small as this courageous action was, it nevertheless aroused such a hurricane of outraged protests on the part of the timber barons that it shook Washington. Commissioner Wilson of the Land Office, who had dared to enforce the law in the teeth of powerful interests and send Willard on his fateful mission, was fired. And it was not until twelve years later, in 1865, that a compromise between the Land Office in Washington and the lumber companies was announced by which lumbering would be permitted on public lands on payment of a "reasonable" fee. (No such fee was ever collected.) The final "solution" to the problem of timber stealing came in the form of the Act of June 15, 1880, which specified that timber poachers would escape prosecution provided they bought the land on which they had trespassed—at a fee of $1.25 an acre.

The tide of greed, waste, and lawlessness did not begin to turn until the formation of the American Forestry Association in 1875. Its foundation was "the first tangible and enduring outgrowth of a growing awareness on the part of the informed public that our renewable resources were not necessarily inexhaustible and that forest use should be accompanied by forest restoration." Its purpose was "to halt indiscriminate forest destruction in America, promote forest protection, and encourage permanent productive use of forest land." It marked the start of a sane commercial forest policy and the first attempt at applying scientific principles to forest management. One of the Association's first tangible effects was its success in persuading Congress to give the President authority to set aside public lands as forest reserves, and on March 30, 1891, President Benjamin Harrison proclaimed the first reserve, Yellowstone Park Timberland. This was the beginning of the national park system.

If any one man could be called "the father of American forestry," he was Gifford Pinchot. His father James, who owned extensive timberlands in Pennsylvania, had been deeply troubled by the ruthlessness and wasteful practices of lumbering. He sent his son to study the science of forestry—what was known of it at that time, and it wasn't very much—in England, France, and Switzerland, since no schools of this kind existed at home.

After his return to the United States he spent a year traveling and lecturing across the country. In December 1891, Pinchot, the first professionally trained American forester, was appointed by George W. Vanderbilt to manage his estate, the 7,000 acre Biltmore Forest in North Carolina. His assignment was to turn a millionaire's hobby into a profitable enterprise by controlling a single forest so that it could continue to produce—a task then considered impossible. Pinchot managed to do the impossible right from the start by applying principles that are still considered the foundation of modern commercial forest management: convince the local population that what you are doing is in their own interest and get their cooperation; practice improvement cutting, i.e., take out trees that are too old, worthless, or deformed so that the desirable young trees can grow up into a good stand of timber; make sure your woodsmen cut timber with the least damage to the remaining trees and take care when removing the logs; fence out cattle, which can do untold damage through overgrazing, trampling down seedling trees, and compacting the porous forest soil; prevent the setting and spreading of fire.

Pinchot's success in managing the Biltmore Forest and placing it on a sustained-yield basis gave a severe jolt to those lumbermen who were convinced that the only way to make money in timber was to "cut and get out." It also gave a badly needed shot in the arm to the small group of conservationists who were already trying to convince their fellow Americans that their timber supply was not inexhaustible. And when, at the Chicago World's Fair of 1893, an exhibition of the Biltmore project was shown complete with models, photographs, and press releases which included the first year's balance sheet, reaction was universally favorable. A turning point in the history of American forestry had been reached.

In 1898, President McKinley appointed Pinchot head of the Forest Division, at that time an obscure branch of the U.S. Department of Agriculture. He became chief forester after the Forestry Division, on July 1, 1901, had been promoted to full bureau status. From then on progress, although at first agonizingly slow, was steady. Following a suggestion by Raphael Zon, one of Pinchot's best foresters, an experimental station was set up in 1908 in the Coconino National Forest in Arizona. Its purpose was to learn more about tree planting and cutting techniques, fire protection, and the role which trees play in maintaining the efficiency of watersheds. This first step toward scientific forest management was followed by the creation in 1910 of a central Forest Products Laboratory in Madison, Wisconsin, which made valuable contributions to wood technology by developing new methods of bleaching kraft pulp, making it suitable to the production of high-grade white bond and printing papers, and by performing pioneer work in new techniques for kiln-drying lumber, wood preservation, and the manufacture of plywood.

By that time, the old hostility between the lumber industry and the federal government was gradually disappearing, and a newly kindled spirit of cooperation manifested itself in the enactment of several laws which were to have far-reaching beneficial consequences. The first of these was the Weeks Law of 1911 which provided for federal-state cooperation in fire control and in protecting forested watersheds on headwaters of navigable rivers. It was the first federal aid law in which the government offered to match state contributions on a 50–50 basis, and it proved to be a great incentive to the installation of woodland fire control systems because, without a federally approved fire-control system, a state was ineligible to receive federal subsidies. The Weeks Law was followed in 1924 by the Clarke-McNary Act which put cooperation between the federal government and the lumber industry on an even broader basis by working toward effective fire-control for all private and state-owned lands. This had been a long overdue necessity because, at that time, 46 per cent of all state and privately owned timberland was still without organized fire control and fires were destroying timber equal to one-fourth of the annual harvest. In addition, the Clarke-McNary Law provided for free distribution of seedling trees to farmers for rehabilitating their wood lots, and a free information service to anyone who requested it. Modern forestry had come of age.

Already in 1920, the Weyerhaeuser Company—today the largest integrated forest products organization in the world, with holdings totaling 3.6 million acres of forest land—during consultation with David T. Mason, a dedicated conservationist, had taken the first tentative steps toward developing a program that eventually would lead to perpetual-yield forestry. Their far-sighted thinking bore fruit on June 12, 1941, when Governor Arthur B. Langlie made the dedicatory speech at the opening of Weyerhaeuser's 120,000 acre "Clemons Tree Farm" near Montesano, Washington, the world's first experiment in sustained-yield forestry.

Tree farming is the direct outgrowth of the Clarke-McNary Law and the 1943 Capital Gains Amendment, Section 117 (K), to the Internal Revenue Code. The Clarke-McNary Law made efficient and relatively inexpensive fire control possible, without which no investor would take the risk of tying up capital for many years in a commodity that at any moment might go up in smoke. And under the 1943 Amendment, the financial yield of stumpage is recognized as capital gains and therefore taxed at a lower rate than ordinary income to compensate for the many years of waiting for trees to grow.

The term "tree farm" is the result of a lucky inspiration: around 1939, when Weyerhaeuser had the problem of protecting a large tract of freshly cut-over land from fires set by berry-pickers and hunters so that a new crop of trees could mature, a local newspaper editor proposed to post signs carrying the words "tree farm." He reasoned that people were less likely to set fire to somebody's farm than to a piece of weed-choked wasteland, and experience has proved him right.

Today, a tree farm is defined as "an area of privately owned taxpaying forest land, protected and managed for repeated crops of forest products," and the sign "Tree Farm—Member American Tree Farming System" has become the respected emblem of progressive forest management. By January 1st, 1967, a total of 31,239 tree farms comprising 70,166,051 acres had been certified by the sponsors of the program, the American Forest Products Industries, Inc., an independent, nonprofit educational organization with headquarters in Washington.

To become eligible for membership in the Tree Farm System, a woodland owner must give assurance that he will raise continuing forest crops for man's use; protect his woods from fire, insects, disease, and destructive grazing; improve his stand of timber periodically by removing weed trees and worthless trees that are crowding out more desirable ones; thin his woods to allow growing room for the remaining trees; harvest his trees when they are ripe and in such a way as to assure another crop; and restock bare or poorly stocked areas to reestablish a productive forest.

Wood and wood products

For all-round utility, and particularly as a building material for residences, temporary structures, interiors, and for making furniture, wood has no equal because no other material combines all the following desirable qualities. Wood is easily worked into various shapes with simple, inexpensive tools requiring comparatively little skill. It is light in weight and therefore easily shipped and handled. It can be conveniently fastened together by nails, screws, bolts, or glue. It is comparatively strong: pound for pound, in regard to compression and bending, certain framing woods are as strong and stiff as fairly good steel and considerably stronger than cast iron; structures made of laminated wood are often preferable to comparable structures made of steel. Wood has low heat conductivity and makes warm buildings. It does not rust and is more resistant to acids, salt water, and other corrosive agents than many other structural materials. It provides smooth, sanitary surfaces, is easily painted or stained, and lends itself well to preservative treatments. And wooden buildings are easily altered or repaired, as openings can be cut and additions made without difficulty.

Since the birth of this nation in 1776, the American lumber industry has produced an estimated 3,000 billion board feet* of lumber. This is enough to build 57 million urban homes, 13 million farmhouses, 2 million schools and libraries, 720,000 churches, and 500,000 factories. In addition, the forests of the United States have produced 6 billion cords of fuel-wood, hundreds of millions of cords of wood for pulp and paper, 450 million telephone poles, 11 billion fence posts, and 10 billion railroad ties.

In 1964, the total lumber consumption of this country was 40 billion 500 million board feet. During that year, 22 per cent of the world's lumber, 57 per cent of its plywood, and about 41 per cent of its paper and paperboard came from American forests. What this means will be more intelligible if one contemplates the following figures, most of which were supplied by Forest Resource Report No. 17, published in February 1965 by the Forest Service of the U.S. Department of Agriculture.

The land area of the continental United States (not counting Alaska) amounts to approximately 1 billion 900 million acres. At the time of arrival of the first settlers, about 43 per cent or 820 million acres were covered by forests, nearly the same amount were grass or range land, and the remainder were mountains or desert. Today, virgin forests are reduced to a mere two per cent of the total land area.

Yet despite all depredations by a timber-hungry nation, of the 2.3 billion acres of land that comprise the 50 states, approximately 33 per cent or 759 million acres are still covered by forests, most of this acreage consisting of second- and third-growth timber. During the last fifty-some years, forest acreage has actually grown, because abandonment of farm land in certain areas and reversion to timber growing has more than offset the loss of forest land due to highway building, utilities rights-of-way, reservoirs, industrial expansion, and urban sprawl. During the decade prior to 1953, for instance, additions to the commercial forest acreage in the 48 contiguous states exceeded withdrawals by 24 million acres, and this increase in forest area continued between 1953 and 1963, although at a slower rate, with a net addition of another 19 million acres to the commercial forest area.

Mature trees for the most part are harvested by one of three methods of cutting: block cutting, the seed tree method, and selective cutting.

In *block cutting* (also called clear cutting), all the trees within a certain area are harvested at one time. Seen from the air, a block-cut forest has a checkerboard appearance, as if Paul Bunyan had snipped large

---

* A board foot is the American lumber industry's standard unit of measurement and is represented by a board one foot long, one foot wide, and one inch thick.

15

squarish patches out of the green mantle of the mountains. These patches are rarely larger, and commonly smaller, than 100 acres each. Block cutting is the method most suitable to forests consisting of even-aged trees, more or less uniform in size, of species that require full sunlight for proper growth and possess a root system so shallow that if scattered seed trees were left, they would be blown over by the wind. Reforestation is often done by helicopters which sow some 40,000 seeds to the acre and can reseed several hundred acres a day. Block cutting is the method most commonly used in the Douglas fir forests of the Northwest.

The *seed tree method* of harvesting is most suited to forests consisting of trees that grow best in full sunlight, with strong and deep roots, whose seeds can be scattered by the wind. Five to ten years before harvest time, well-developed healthy trees spaced at fairly even intervals are selected to become the future seed trees. Nearby trees are removed so that the seed trees will receive more light and water which in turn will stimulate growth and seed production. At harvest time, all the other trees are cut while the seed trees are left standing. Wind will scatter their seeds, the cut-over area will reforest itself, and when the new tree crop is well established, the seed trees themselves can be harvested. This is the method most commonly used in the pine forests of the Southeast.

Selective cutting is best suited to forests consisting of trees of different species which also vary in age and size and grow well in partial shade. Under this system, no large area is ever completely cleared of trees; instead, scattered mature trees are cut either individually or in small groups and harvested periodically. Younger trees are left undisturbed for future growth and seed production. This method can be used to harvest trees that have either deep or shallow root systems and whose seeds are not necessarily distributed by the wind. It is commonly practiced in the Northern red spruce, the Northeastern hardwood, and the Western ponderosa pine and redwood forests.

Lumbering is a dangerous job requiring muscle, experience, and skill, and it has a cast of characters all its own. Hardhatted "fallers" working in pairs use power saws to cut down the trees selected by professional foresters, who also determine the cutting pattern best suited to foster reforestation. Each tree is cut as close to the ground as possible to avoid waste, and the direction of its fall is carefully controlled so as not to damage remaining trees and to prevent the harvested tree from shattering itself in the fall. "Buckers" remove the limbs from the fallen tree and saw the trunk into manageable sections. The logs are removed to the loading place either by dragging them with a tractor driven by a "catskinner," or on aerial cables strung from a portable spar, a tall rigged steel pole which works off a yarding machine that reels in the steel cable and winds it on a drum. From the top of the spar, steel cables reach deep into the forest to the logging area where "choker setters" attach the logs to the aerial tramway with cable chokers under the direction of the "rigging slinger," the boss who supervises this operation. The log securely fastened, he then signals the "whistle punk" who, either by field telephone or walkie-talkie radio, relays the command to the yarding machine operator at the other end of the line to start hauling in the logs. At the loading place, "chasers" receive the logs and take them off the cable. The logs are then lifted by crane and loaded on a truck trailer, secured with chains, and driven off to the sawmill where they are dumped into the millpond. Storing the logs in water facilitates sorting, protects the wood from end checking and attacks by wood-boring insects, and reduces the danger of fire. Here the logs remain, often for weeks, until they go under the saw.

Modern wood technology is constantly searching for new ways to increase the degree of utilization of the substance of a tree. During the early 1900's, only 30 per cent or less of the average cut tree was converted into useful products. Small, crooked, or defective logs, tree tops, branches, limbs, and high stumps were left unused in the woods to rot. Slabs—the bark-covered outside boards—as well as edgings and trimmings from the sawed planks were used for fuel or merely piled up and burned.

Today about 70 per cent of each harvested tree is utilized. Felling trees with power instead of hand saws makes it possible to cut closer to the ground, leaving less wood in the stumps. In the mill, thinner-gauge saws reduce the volume of sawdust and thereby save many board feet of lumber. Before logs are made into lumber, the bark is often removed so that all unused slabs, trimmings, and edgings may be cut into small chips and made into pulp for paper or pressed wood products. Bark is sometimes converted into insulating material or used in roofing felts and soil conditioners. Much sawdust is utilized in the manufacture of wood flour for plastics, compressed into fuel logs and briquettes, or converted to pulp. Naval stores—turpentine and pitch—as well as nitrocellulose, used in making dynamite, are obtained from Southern pine stumps. Newly developed glues and methods of lamination can make larger pieces out of many small ones. Even knotholes can be filled by machine to turn former leftover wood into useful products.

In addition, many tree species formerly regarded as useless "weed trees" can now be used for commercial purposes. Larch, cottonwood, and the true firs of the West have become accepted lumber material. Aspen and red alder and various other hardwoods once considered weeds are now important species for pulp. Furthermore, in addition to the *harvest cut* of mature trees, a number of other cuts are now carried out regularly in well-managed forests to obtain more complete utilization of available resources. *Thinning*, for example, has become economical because smaller diameter trees cut to thin the forest can be made into utility poles, posts, piling, and pulp-wood. The same applies to *pre-logging*, i.e., removal of smaller trees which might be damaged or destroyed during the main harvest. During *re-logging* operations, a second crop is gathered by removing trees purposely left untouched while harvesting the first. In *salvage logging*, all usable logs, tree tops, and wood chunks left during the main operation are picked up with special equipment. In hardwood forests, large limbs are gathered for use as fuelwood or fence posts or conversion into charcoal. And periodic removal of insect-attacked or diseased trees permits utilization before they die on the stump.

Harvested wood takes many forms. The most important of these is the sawlog—a log large enough to be made into lumber or used in the manufacture of plywood. About 70 per cent of the annual wood crop goes into sawlogs. The annual per capita consumption of lumber in the United States reached its peak in 1905 when it amounted to 507 board feet. Since then, per capita consumption has declined and stood in 1966 at 211 board feet. On the other hand, plywood consumption climbed from per capita rate of 10¹/₂ square feet in 1940 to nearly 86 square feet by 1965.

Next in volume to sawlogs is pulpwood, the primary raw material for paper and paper products, which comprises about 27 per cent of the tree harvest. Unlike lumber use, per capita consumption of paper and paper products has been rising sharply, climbing from 249 pounds in 1943 to 531 pounds in 1966.

In addition to the three major categories of wood utilization—lumber, plywood, and pulp—other important forest products such as insulation board, particleboard, and hardboard are made from leftover material resulting from the manufacture of lumber or plywood and from small diameter logs. Utility poles, piles, fence posts, flagpoles, railroad ties, shingles, cooperage, charcoal, and fuelwood are other important products, and a large number of silvichemicals—chemicals derived from wood—are acquiring more and more importance in the manufacture of increasingly sophisticated products.

Forest products are processed in four main types of plants: sawmills, plywood mills, pulp mills, and wood distillation plants.

The *sawmill* is the main tool of the forest products industry. During the first 200 years of its existence, the U.S. lumber industry's output came from small, crudely built sawmills powered by hand or water. Their output went almost entirely into the houses, furniture, barns, bridges, and other structures needed by people living nearby, or into locally built boats and ships. A few mills made lumber for export to Europe. As the population increased, larger sawmills were built, particularly after 1830 when steam power was introduced in sawmill operation. These larger mills produced more lumber than local populaces could consume, and lumber merchants bought up their surplus for resale outside the community. Transporting lumber and lumber products became a major source of revenue for the country's railroads and shipping lines. However, as the immense stands of old-growth timber decreased, the large mills diminished in number and gave way again to smaller mills more suitable to processing second-growth stands of trees. Today, mills which produce under 10 million board feet per year apiece account for nearly two-thirds of our annual lumber output, which in 1966 stood at 37.1 billion board feet.

After World War II, the one-purpose sawmill turning out a single product—lumber—began to fade out of the picture, giving way to the integrated mill of today, which is more economical because it makes use of material formerly considered waste. An integrated mill consists essentially of two or more plants on the same site. Logs delivered to an integrated mill are carefully examined and sorted according to species, size, and quality before they are moved on to one of various departments, which may be 1) the log barker, 2) one or more sawmills complete with speciality mill and remanufacturing plant, 3) a plywood or veneer plant, 4) a hardboard plant, 5) a chipping plant, and 6) a pulp or paper mill.

The integrated sawmill is a highly mechanized industrial complex. In all phases of production, machines now do the work once performed by straining oxen and sweating men. Logs are pulled lengthwise out of the millpond by a power-driven "bull chain" or "jack ladder." At many mills, hydraulic or mechanical barkers remove all bark from the logs to facilitate sawing and permit economic salvage of trimmings and slabs for pulpwood. The bark is then available for manufacture into other products or for burning to produce steam and power. After debarking, logs are hauled onto the sawing deck where they are stored before being rolled onto the "carriage"—a wheel-equipped platform on rails which carries the log back and forth past the headsaw which cuts it into "cants" or "flitches"—logs with two or four of their rounded outer surfaces or "slabs" removed so that they are no longer round but flat on two or four sides. A further operation brings the cant to the "gang saw"—circular blades lined side by side just a plank's thickness apart—which slices the cants into boards. Farther along the production line, an "edger" saws the boards into the desired widths and a "trimmer" cuts them to the proper length. From here they go by conveyer belt—the "green chain," green referring not to color but to the sap moisture of the freshly cut wood—into the sorting shed where trained workmen grade each board. The next step is seasoning or drying—the lumber is stacked in a yard, each piece carefully separated by narrow strips of wood to permit free air circulation throughout the entire stack; or it is kiln dried, i.e., stacked in a heated chamber under controlled conditions of temperature, air velocity, and relative humidity. Finally, the dry but still rough lumber is given a smooth surface by planing—passing it through a set of rotating knives; then it is graded again before being shipped to the wholesale lumber dealer.

The main products of a sawmill are: *timbers*, massive pieces of lumber used in heavy construction work: barns, bridges, churches, docks, factories, heavy scaffolding, ships and tugs, etc.; *construction lumber*, wood for beams, boards, boat hulls and parts, concrete forms, joists, planks, rafters, sills, studs, walls, etc.; *finished lumber*, primarily baseboards, casings, lath, paneling, siding, stepping, etc.; *remanufactured lumber*, which includes a virtually endless array of products from baseball bats and butcher blocks to furniture, gunstocks, and musical instruments; *ties*, mainly railroad cross ties; *cooperage*, barrels, buckets, cooling towers for industrial air-conditioners, silos, tanks, tubs, etc.; *miscellaneous products* such as corncribs, dunnage, fence pickets, flagpoles, posts, shingles, tunnel and mine props, utility and telephone poles, etc.; and *residues* such as bark, fuelwood, planer shavings, and sawdust.

The *plywood mill* produces plywood and veneer. Total plywood consumption in the United States in 1965 ($^3/_8$-inch base) was approximately 17 billion square feet, about three-quarters of which was softwood. Softwood plywood is used primarily as a building material, especially for residential construction. The main use of hardwood plywood is for paneling and containers. Most of the high-grade hardwood veneer is used in furniture; low grades are used for making egg crates, berry baskets, and the like.

Plywood is a wood-and-glue "sandwich" consisting of an odd number of layers of veneer—thin slices of wood—assembled in such a way that the grain of each layer or ply runs at right angles to the grain of the adjacent ply. This type of construction gives plywood three structural advantages over ordinary boards: 1) It does not split. As anyone knows who has ever driven a nail into a thin board or has cleaved firewood with an ax, wood splits easily with the grain but it is virtually impossible to split against the grain. Crossing layers of wood, as is done in plywood, eliminates the tendency to split. 2) It is dimensionally more stable. With variations in moisture content, wood can change dimension up to 12 per cent across the grain whereas the maximal dimensional change along the grain is rarely more than one per cent. The cross-layer principle equalizes such changes so that the maximum dimensional change either across or with the grain is generally not over two per cent. 3) Plywood is flexible. Thin layers of wood bend easily without breaking. As a result, plywood is particularly adapted to bending, curving, and forming, as evidenced by a multitude of curved plywood products such as chair backs and seats, boat hulls, bowling alley gullies, domes, and many others.

Plywood manufacturing utilizes the log more completely than lumber manufacturing. Since most plywood veneers are produced by slicing against a knife, no sawdust results and a larger part of the log is converted into the desired product. Plywood also makes for more efficient utilization of rare and valuable woods because low-grade veneers can be used for the inner plies—the core—and only the face veneer needs to consist of the more valuable wood.

Veneer can be cut in four ways: 1) By rotary lathe. The debarked log is clamped in a huge lathe and rotated against the edge of a long stationary knife which peels off the wood spirally in a continuous thin sheet. Between 80 and 90 per cent of all veneer is cut by this method. 2) By slicing. A flitch is attached to a log bed which moves it up and down against a stationary knife. At each downward stroke, a thin rectangular piece of veneer is sliced off the flitch. This method is used mainly to cut face veneer of hardwood logs such as mahogany, walnut, cherry, and oak. 3) By stay log cutting. A "bolt"—a log cut lengthwise—is attached to a metal beam or "stay log" mounted off-center in a lathe and rotated against a knife edge. This method, a combination of rotary cutting and slicing, produces individual sheets of half-round veneer which are primarily used for faces. 4) By sawing. A circular saw with a thin blade cuts thin slices off a flitch. This method is mainly used to achieve special grain effects in oak and cedar face veneers.

Veneer sheets are cut to desired lengths and widths by a mechanical "clipper" and dried in huge oven-like dryers. They subsequently go to a glue spreader where they are coated on both sides with a liquid glue. A number of sheets are then put together in the form of a sandwich with the grain of each sheet at right angles to that of the next. Finally, the entire sandwich goes into a powerful press in which it remains until the glue has set. The emerging panel is then trimmed, sanded, inspected, graded, strapped, and shipped to the lumber dealer.

The *pulp mill* converts pulpwood, sawmill slabs, veneer cores, and wood chips into pulp, the raw material for paper, paperboard, rayon, wood cellulose, and a number of other products. Production of pulp and paper increased 850 per cent in the past fifty years, reaching an all-time high in 1966 when 5,271 paper-making and converting plants in the United States consumed a total of 56 million cords of pulpwood weighing some 160 million tons. Annual per capita consumption of paper products in the United States in 1966 was 531 pounds, more than four times as high as the corresponding European figure.

The first step in pulp manufacture is to break down wood into its basic constituents: cellulose fibers, a glue-like cement called lignin which binds these fibers together, and lesser quantities of sugars, gums, resins, and mineral salts. The fibers are then separated from the other materials, rearranged in new patterns, and in combination with other substances made into a different product.

Depending on the type of wood and the requirements of the end product, pulping can be done either mechanically or chemically. In mechanical pulping, the debarked logs are reduced to fibers by huge, rough-faced grinding stones to become ground pulp. Since this method does not remove the lignin, papers made of groundwood pulp generally do not keep their whiteness and strength as long as papers made from chemical pulp but eventually become brown and brittle. On the other hand, the low cost of groundwood paper makes it preferable for newsprint, lower grades of tablet paper, and other papers which do not require unusual strength or durability.

In chemical pulping, wood fibers are separated from their lignin binder by cooking in any one of several chemical solutions, primarily sulphite, soda, or sulphate. Paper made from hardwoods through the soda process is noted for its fine texture and excellent printing qualities, making it particularly suited for high-grade magazine and book papers. The sulphate process is used mainly for pulping both softwoods and hardwoods for kraft papers used for wrappings, grocery bags, and other durable products requiring strength. Special sulphite and sulphate pulps called dissolving pulps are used in the manufacture of cellophane, explosives, plastics, and rayon.

In semi-chemical pulping, mechanical and chemical methods combine to manufacture a pulp particularly suitable for corrugated paperboard and other items requiring stiffness and resilience.

In each of the chemical methods, pulpwood sticks must be chipped before they are cooked. Rotating knives slice across the log, cutting off chips from $3/8$ to $1^3/8$ inches long and about $1/8$ inch thick. An endless conveyer belt carries these chips to storage tanks above chemical vats called digesters. These digesters operate on the same principle as a kitchen pressure cooker. Wood chips in chemical solution are cooked with steam until reduced to a wet, pulpy mass. It is this cooking which dissolves the resins and glue-like lignin and causes the fibers to separate.

No matter how it is produced, wood pulp requires additional treatment before it can be made into paper or paper products. Washing removes nonfibrous substances and undesirable chemicals; screening removes dirt as well as uncooked or unbroken pieces of wood, and separates fibers according to size; bleaching further refines the pulp and gives it the desired degree of whiteness. Finally—unless the pulp is going to be used immediately—most of the water must be extracted from the screened stock, which then is made into sheets, bundled, and shipped to a paper mill.

At the paper mill, the first step is to mix the pulp with water in a large tank called a beater. Often, two or more kinds of pulp must be combined to produce papers with specific qualities. Newsprint, for example, is made chiefly of groundwood pulp to which small quantities of chemical pulp are added to give additional strength. In the beater, the fibers in the diluted pulp are separated, and glue-like materials called "color" and "size" are added as needed, together with a filler. From the beater the pulp goes to the "Jordan," a machine in which sets of metal bars or knives rub against the fibers, separating them, reducing them to proper length, and fraying them so that, when water is drained from them on the paper machine, they will combine to form a uniform sheet of paper.

From the Jordan the pulp goes into a storage chest and from there onto the "Fourdrinier," a machine named in honor of the Fourdrinier brothers, Henry and Sealy, who perfected the paper-making machine invented in 1798 by the Frenchman Nicholas-Louis Robert. When the pulp runs onto the endless wire-mesh screen of the Fourdrinier, it consists of about 99 per cent water. Constant side-to-side vibration of the screen, which has about 6,000 tiny holes per square inch, causes the cellulose fibers to become interlaced, a process during which much water is lost, leaving a still wet sheet of pulp. This sheet is further dried by suction that pulls water down through the screen into tanks below.

Pulp for paperboard is processed in cylinder machines instead of on a moving flat screen. A number of wire-covered cylinders revolve in vats containing fibers suspended in water. The fibers collect on the screens as the water flows through, and a multi-ply sheet of paperboard is formed.

From the screen, or from the wire-covered cylinders, the wet sheet of pulp passes to a belt of wool felt which carries it through many pairs of heavy rollers where more water is pressed out or absorbed by the felt. Now strong enough to sustain its own weight, the fast-moving sheet of paper or paperboard leaves the woolen felt and enters the dry end of the paper machine. Here it is dried by traveling over a number of rotating, steam-heated steel cylinders on a path that may be as short as twenty feet for cigarette papers or as long as 350 feet for some types of heavy wrapping paper. On these dry rollers, sometimes as wide as twenty-five feet and over which the paper moves at speeds of up to 2,600 feet per minute, nearly all the water is removed.

Most papers go through one or more additional finishing processes. One of these is an ironing process called calendering in which the paper passes through sets of heavy polished steel rollers to further improve the smoothness of its surface. In another process, stacks of cut sheets of paper interleaved alternatingly with sheets of linen cloth are fed into a huge press which gives the emerging paper a linen finish. By treating paper with wax, polyethylene, asphalt, starch, and other materials, moisture-resistant types are made, including a variety of paper containers for liquids such as the familiar milk cartons and paper cups.

Wood distillation and hydrolysis plants form the fourth and last major group of forest product plants. Their raw materials are the leftovers from sawmills and pulp mills: slabs, edgings, trimmings, and sawdust, to which are added thin roundwood bolts and the crooked logs, limbs, branches, and stumps which neither sawmill nor pulp mill can use. Such "scavenger plants" process the last recoverable scrap of a tree into some useful product.

Distillation is the process of driving off gases or vapors from liquids or solids by heat and pressure in a retort or still, and condensing the resultant products. Hydrolysis is a chemical process of decomposition involving addition of the elements of water.

Typical products of wood distillation plants are such well-known chemicals as acetic acid, a solvent used in the production of rayon, cellulose acetate, photographic films, lacquers, plastics, and perfumes; acetone, a solvent which is used in making explosives among other things; methanol, best known for its use in antifreeze solutions, as a dry-cleaning agent, and as a component of paints, varnishes, and shellacs; cedar oil, tar oil (creosote), pine oil, and turpentine; dipentene, a solvent for reclaiming old rubber; and charcoal, used primarily in water purification and whisky making, for barbecue fires and artists' sketching sticks. Typical products of wood hydrolysis plants are acetic acid, carbolic acid, ethyl alcohol, glycerine, butadiene (synthetic rubber), oxalic acid, pyrogallol, resins, and lignin powder for plastics and laminates.

The paper industry is no less waste-conscious than the lumber industry, and large quantities of pulp for certain types of paperboard are made up of re-pulped waste paper from which ink and other impurities have been removed. As a matter of fact, more than one-fourth of the fibrous raw material of all paper and paperboard production in the United States comes from waste paper. Even the spent liquids left over from the chemical pulping processes are reprocessed and the yields used in making adhesives, road binders, tanning agents, plastics, dyes, rosin soap, acetic acid, turpentine, fertilizer and many other products.

A number of tree products fit into none of the previous categories. There is, for example, *fuelwood*, consumption of which has been declining steadily since the last century when it was an important source of energy for locomotives, steamships, and industrial power plants as well as for heating and cooking. In 1952, for example, the total fuelwood consumption in the United States was estimated at 58½ million cords, but by 1966 it had dropped to an estimated 15 million. No figures are available for *sawdust*, but its uses are many: absorbent for explosives, composition flooring, filler for linoleum, fireworks, handsoaps, molded products, in butcher shops, ice storage, insulation, livestock bedding, meat smoking, packing, soil conditioning, and wood flour for making bowling balls, among others. Even lowly *bark* is used, chiefly as insulating material, for fuel, and in the manufacture of glues, plastics,

mulch, fertilizer, soil conditioner, and roofing felts. The bark of some trees also furnishes important ingredients for dyes (osage orange and black oak), drugs (slippery elm), tannins (hemlock, chestnut, oak), and spices (cinnamon tree). *Saps* and *gums* are collected from V-shaped incisions cut into the bark of living trees and play important roles in the manufacture of rubber (latex from rubber trees), turpentine (pine), maple syrup and maple sugar (sugar maple), birch beer, Canada balsam (balsam fir), and other products. *Edible tree fruits* support entire industries: the Florida and California citrus fruits; peaches, apples and pears, cherries and plums; avocados and pomegranates; bananas; walnuts, pecans, and other nuts. And finally, there are *Christmas trees*, mostly Scotch pine, balsam and Douglas fir, black and white spruce, some 40 million of which are cut annually to bring into the American home a breath of the wild woods at least once a year.

The number of people throughout the world is increasing at an alarming rate. Paralleling this population growth is a corresponding increase in demands for forest products. In 1963, according to the last Census of Manufacturers made by the U.S. Department of Commerce, 32,000 sawmills, 360 pulp mills, 800 paper and paperboard mills, and 511 plywood and veneer mills were competing with one another for their share of raw materials, most of which had to come from American forests. Despite these heavy demands the total forest area of the United States has actually increased during the last fifty years, testifying to the degree that scientific forest management as manifested in modern methods of tree cutting, disease and pest control, forest fire prevention, tree planting, and reforestation, has made possible the rise in productivity of our commercial forests. This gratifying result has been achieved through the application of two principles: research and conservation. Research led to new and better methods for growing trees and to valuable discoveries in wood technology; conservation pointed the way to more efficient utilization of our far from unlimited sylvan resources. It is hoped that these principles will continue to guide our forest industry, for, as the U.S. Forest Service has put it so well, "Forestry is not a short-time proposition. Where this nation stands in timber supply in the year 2000 will depend largely on actions taken during the next two decades."

The ecological role of trees

It was a beautiful morning in June when my wife and I left Garberville, California, and drove north on US 101 toward Dyerville to revisit the towering redwoods and take photographs for this book (see picture pages 77–80). An azure vault spanned a bright and glittering world, and along the ridges, the spires of the great trees cut dark and sharp into the sky. The sun was already hot but the air still cool as we drove in a spirit of pleasant anticipation along the twisting road that follows the Eel River toward Humboldt Redwoods State Park and entered the whispering silence of the forest. And then, suddenly, something went wrong. Unexpectedly, our mood changed. Elation gave way to gloom as we penetrated deeper into the woods; for the woods were gray. The columns of the immense trunks, which we remembered as cinnamon brown, were gray. The ground, which should have been covered by brown needles and green moss, saplings and ferns, was a tangle of broken sticks and branches uniformly coated with a gray film of silt. What evil had befallen this great forest to make it look as if just risen from the bottom of a muddy lake? Our question was answered a few miles further down the road when we came upon a white board nailed to the gray trunk of a tree, commemorating the height—thirty-five feet!—at which the catastrophic flood of December 1964 had stood above the forest floor—a flood which had devastated the Pacific Northwest to the tune of three-quarters of a billion dollars.

The primary cause of most floods is excessive deforestation of watersheds—the region surrounding the headwaters of a river. A watershed can be as small as the upland drainage of a farm pond or as large as the Mississippi River basin. No matter what its size, it is from a watershed that a river gets its water supply, and what happens here can affect places a thousand miles away.

Without water, life cannot exist; 100 pounds of wood contain seven to eight gallons of water; but during the time it takes this wood to grow, about 1,000 times that much water is needed to keep the life processes of the tree going—a tree in full foliage may consume a ton of water a day. The present per capita water consumption in the United States is 60 gallons a day, and it is expected to rise to 85 gallons within the next thirty-five years—and by that time the population of this country will have doubled. Farms need water for people, animals, and crops; homes need it for drinking, washing, and cooking. Towns and cities require water for firefighting, sanitation, and recreation. Industry must have water to generate power and light, for use as a solvent, in cooling and waste disposal, or as part of the finished product. For people in civilized countries, obtaining water seems simple: a turn of the faucet, and it flows. But the faucet must be fed by a pipe and the pipe by a conduit connected to a reservoir or a lake which in turn must be supplied by a brook or stream which gets its water from a watershed.

Too much water in the watershed is nearly as bad as too little. When heavy rains and melting snow turn brooks into torrents that swell placid streams into raging rivers, entire communities are flooded, families driven from their homes, bridges washed away, and transportation brought to a standstill. Not a year goes by that we don't read about disastrous floods somewhere in the world. In the spring of 1948, the Columbia River went on a rampage in the course of which forty people lost their lives and 60,000 were left homeless. In 1952, the Mississippi River flooded its basin and caused some 100 million dollars of damage to farmland alone. And it will take a long time before the 1955 New England floods, which destroyed property valued at a billion dollars, are forgotten. These are only the big, catastrophic, headline-making floods affecting hundreds of square miles. Much more often, a torrential storm over a small drainage area causes only a local flood which destroys the land or crops of only a few farms or inundates the streets of a small town. But because they are so numerous, collectively such floods from minor streams cause more damage than the spectacular ones. In the United States alone, the losses from all floods are estimated to average about a billion dollars per year. The main cause of most of these floods—and losses—is man's abuse of his watershed lands.

To understand the relationship between watershed and water supply it is necessary to know whence water comes and where it goes. Everyone knows that water falls from the clouds as rain or snow. Less commonly known is the fact that this phenomenon is only part of a huge worldwide circulatory process called the water cycle which goes on endlessly within the atmosphere. For although the earth's water supply is limited and finite, and although humans, animals, and plants constantly use enormous quantities of water, not a single drop is ever lost, and the available supply always remains constant. The explanation of this apparent paradox lies in the fact that living organisms give off as much water as they take in, and water precipitated to the ground eventually returns to the atmosphere through evaporation.

upon watershed land that nourishes the creeks feeding the streams that combine to form the rivers carrying the water back to the sea whence it is recycled—the water that in passing can sustain man or destroy him and his creations.

Precipitation falling upon a watershed disperses itself in four ways. A small part of the water evaporates from the surfaces of rocks and plants. Another part will hardly penetrate the ground before it is taken up by

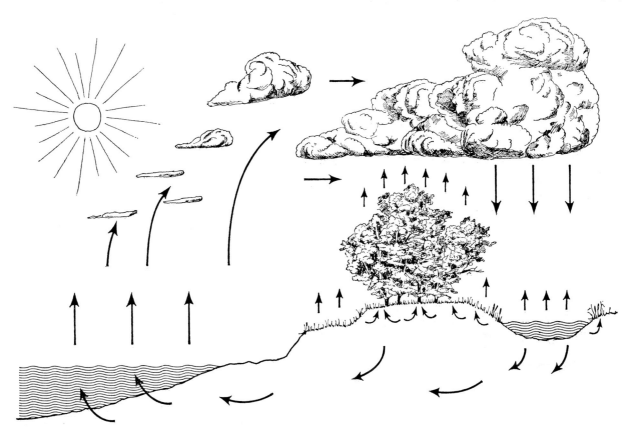

This, in brief, is the water cycle: Under the influence of solar heat, water in the form of vapor rises from the surfaces of oceans, lakes and streams, damp earth and living things, is lifted into the atmosphere, ascends to cooler heights where it is condensed into clouds, drifts with the winds, and cools off to be precipitated again as rain, hail, sleet, or snow. Two-thirds of this water falls back into the seas whence most of it came and is unavailable for use by terrestrial organisms. Large quantities are immediately taken up by plants, farm crops, grasses, and trees and in time returned to the atmosphere through transpiration without ever having fed a single creek or stream. It is the water that falls

the roots of trees and plants and eventually returned to the air through transpiration. Some water will sink deeply into the soil and, in the form of groundwater, become part of the immense subterranean reservoir that feeds all springs and streams. And some of the water may stay on the surface and run off to lower ground, particularly if the downpour was very heavy or the ground stony and hard.

Of the four courses which precipitating water can take, the last two are of the greatest interest to man: only water that sinks deeply into the earth to become groundwater can maintain the even flow of creeks and streams; water that stays on the surface causes floods.

23

Whether precipitation becomes groundwater or surfacewater depends primarily on the condition of the watershed. And it is here that trees play one of their most important roles in the cyclic web of life because a watershed that is covered by trees can absorb many times the amount of precipitation a treeless watershed could retain.

Rain falling on a treeless watershed strikes the unprotected ground with the full force of the storm. Individual drops hit like little bombs, gouging, beating, and battering the soil, lifting and splashing it back and forth, churning it into a pasty mud that rapidly fills and clogs the pores and passages through which water might enter the soil. Soon the badly compacted ground can no longer absorb the overflow which now collects on the surface and, if the surface is sloping as is usually the case, races downhill in millions of little currents. These combine to become torrents of water that deeply gouge and gully the hillsides, taking with them large amounts of topsoil, gravel, and stones, and dumping their spoils into reservoirs or blanketing low-lying farm land with choking layers of silt.

The great flood of 1966 which devastated Florence and Venice is a classical example of the danger which excessive deforestation of watersheds creates for lower-lying lands. Italy's topography is two-fifths mountains, two-fifths hills, and one-fifth plains. Centuries of ruthless deforestation to provide timber, firewood, and farm land have stripped all but one-fifth of her mountains and hills of their protective forest cover. Italy today with its long spine of mostly treeless mountains is like a house with a steep roof, no gutters, and narrow strips of lawn—the coastal lowlands. During heavy storms, the denuded watersheds can absorb only a small part of the rain, most of which runs unimpeded off the "roof" and inundates the "lawns," the coastal farms, fields, and towns.

The same misuse of land that increases the danger of floods is also largely responsible for water shortages. When water from rain or snow is not stored in the ground but runs off quickly, there is no reserve to keep springs, streams, and lakes supplied during the drier season. As a result, communities that have rashly deforested their watersheds usually suffer from too much water when the snow melts or after heavy rain, and too little during the rest of the year.

Quite a different situation prevails when the watershed is covered by forest. Foliage and branches of trees and shrubs break the force of the falling raindrops, and a resilient mat of moss, dead leaves, twigs, and partly decomposed plant material protects the ground and prevents the soil from being splashed about. Beneath this forest litter, the earth is soft and spongy because it is richly mixed with organic matter and honeycombed with innumerable channels made by roots and burrowing animals, earthworms, insect larvae, and fungi. This biological activity, largely lacking in unprotected land, keeps the soil porous and gives it a crumb-like structure, ideal for storing large quantities of water. This kind of ground will absorb water quickly and hold as much as 35 per cent of its total volume. Rain trickling from the trees to the forest floor will slowly seep into the interstices of the soil, penetrate deeply into the ground, and in time percolate into the groundwater reservoir to emerge at lower levels in the form of seepage, springs, and streams, often even during the driest season.

Snow accumulation and melting are also influenced by forest cover. Although less snow will accumulate in dense coniferous forests than on treeless land, the snow on the forest floor, where it is protected from sun and wind, will stay from one to five weeks longer in spring than on an open site. Snow melting will be delayed, flowing of high streams in early spring reduced, and more water released later when it is most needed. In addition, the loose, porous, and frequently unfrozen forest soil absorbs greater quantities of melting snow than the more tightly packed and usually frozen soil of unprotected land.

The purity of water is almost sɐ important as its quantity. No water surpasses in crystal clarity that of a purling mountain stream that has its source in the forest. This clarity is the result of the extensive filtration which rainwater undergoes during its subterranean passage before it again emerges as a spring. The porous rocks and layers of sand and gravel through which groundwater percolates remove impurities as effectively as the best man-made filters.

On the other hand, creeks and streams fed by surface run-off water always carry with them a large quantity of soil. It is only too well known that most of our rivers are polluted to such a degree that their water is unfit for human use. Although a high degree of this pollution is due to human agencies—primarily sewage, household detergents, industrial wastes, and drainage from mines and oil wells—the biggest pollutant of water is silt. Silt is loose sedimentary material, minute rock particles less than $1/400$ inch in diameter, which are small enough to float suspended in water. Silt-laden water, which is all but useless without expensive treatment, can easily be recognized by the muddy yellow-brown color of the particles of soil it carries. Once carried in suspension by a river, this soil is forever lost to man. The extent of this loss can be gauged from a report by the U.S. Soil Conservation Service: "Careful estimates based on actual measurements indicate that soil losses by erosion from all lands in the United States total 5,400,000,000 tons annually. From farm lands alone, the annual loss is about 3 billion tons, enough to fill a freight train which would girdle the globe 18 times... In a normal production year, erosion by wind and water removes 21 times as much plant food from the soil as is removed in the crops sold off the land... Total cost to the U.S. as the result of uncontrolled erosion and water run-off is estimated at 3 billion 844 million dollars annually."

More than half the waterflow in streams of the United States has its source in forest lands. Proper forest management can keep soil erosion down to a minimum. But even within forests erosion can reach dangerous proportions if vegetation cover has been destroyed through overgrazing by cattle or overbrowsing by deer; if herds of animals or crowds of recreation seekers have compacted the ground and seriously impaired its ability to take up water; or if faulty logging practices prevail.

Trees are the guardians of water and soil. Where trees protect the ground, soil erosion is normally slowed down to a pace equaling that at which new soil is formed by weathering processes and accumulation of dead organic matter. Land covered by virgin forest retains its productivity indefinitely because no vegetation is permanently removed. Dead trees and plants slowly sink into the ground and return their minerals to the soil to be recycled as new trees and plants grow up.

This pattern of continuity changes drastically with the arrival of man. When man occupies the land, he usually does so with the purpose of cultivating it and removing the products of his harvest. And in the course of time, the ground is denuded, domesticated animals destroy the grass, fertility of the soil declines. Accelerated erosion sets in as the ground is increasingly exposed to the elements. Water and wind carry soil from the uplands to the lowlands, burying the rich alluvial farm land. Further winds and rains strip away the earth cover, leaving the fields a stony waste strewn with rocks and boulders. Gullying sets in, and eventually the land becomes useless for cultivation. This is what happened in forested New England, which was largely changed to pasture as the productivity of the soil declined, after more than a century of intensive cultivation. Today it is again two-thirds forest, but of such poor quality that it yields less than 10 per cent of the total rural income. According to estimates by the U.S. Soil Conservation Service, 282 million acres of land within the United States have been either ruined or severely damaged by soil erosion and an additional 755 million acres have lost from one-fourth to three-fourths of their topsoil. Fifty million acres of farm land have been abandoned.

Similar conditions can be observed in many other parts of the world. The cycle is invariably the same: large-scale destruction of trees to provide farm land, lumber, and firewood; cultivation of land unsuitable to cultivation, or cultivation by unsuitable practices such as uphill plowing instead of plowing along the contour, or planting of crops that soon exhaust the soil; change from exhausted farm land to pasture followed by overgrazing; rampant erosion leading to abandonment; and resumption of deforestation to clear additional ground.

Already in 1830, the great geologist Charles Lyell realized that man must be considered "among the powers of organic nature" because of his ability to change the physical geography of the earth. This change began in antiquity and has continued at an ever increasing pace. For example, in prehistoric times, the littoral of the Mediterranean Sea from Spain to the Middle East was densely covered by trees. But the same ruthless deforestation that brought untold wealth to Babylon and Nineveh, to Greece and Rome, in the end contributed to the downfall of their civilizations as the denuded hills eroded, alternating floods and droughts destroyed the fertility of the lowlands, rivers silted up, and coast lines changed, leaving the vitally important harbors dry while the rich organic topsoil swept past on muddy waters out to sea. Today, finally aware of the tragic folly of their ancestors, the peoples of these semi-desert countries wage a desperate battle to bring back the fertility of their lands by replanting their stony watersheds with trees. But the struggle is heartbreaking and the outcome uncertain because the life-giving topsoil is gone and virtually impossible to replace. It will take many lifetimes before new trees will cover the all-important heights and the slow process of topsoil formation can begin all over again.

I said in the beginning that, should the trees die, it is not impossible that man too would become extinct. What then might have seemed a rash and sweeping statement should now acquire new meaning. For trees, as we have seen, are the guardians of water and topsoil—two vital necessities for the existence of plants. Plants, in turn, are vital prerequisites for the existence of man. This is so because every molecule of living substance is built around atoms of carbon. But whereas plants can secure their needed carbon supply directly from the air, man can obtain this vital element only through eating plants, or eating animals that have been feeding on plants. And so the cycle comes back full turn because plants cannot live without an adequate supply of water and topsoil which largely depends on the presence of trees.

Topsoil, or loam, is a precious substance easily damaged or lost. There are many kinds of loam, all different, yet alike in certain important characteristics. Good loams have a loose and porous structure which enables them to store large quantities of water and air. They are honeycombed with the tunnels of earthworms, insect larvae, ants, and moles which provide additional aeration. They are alive with biological activity, bacteria, fungi, and molds, and rich in dead organic matter. And they contain the nutrients and minerals which plants require for healthy growth: nitrogen, phosphorous, magnesium, and potassium as well as the equally important trace-elements, those substances without which plants cannot live although they require them only in the most minute amounts: iron, zinc, copper, manganese, molybdenum, and boron.

The thickness of this precious layer of loam varies considerably but it is rarely very great. Estimates are hardly more than guesses. According to the best authorities, though, the average thickness of topsoil computed for the entire earth is somewhat less than one foot. For the United States, it is somewhere between seven and eight inches. Experts say that it takes probably from 100 to over 1,000 years to build

a single inch of loam—a century may not be long enough to produce one-tenth of an inch. But on these few unique inches depends the existence of all terrestrial organisms, from the lowliest bacterium to man. Beneath this thin layer, nothing breathes, moves, or grows. The lifegiving film that covers the underlying layers of sterile sediments, clays, and rocks is indeed almost frighteningly thin.

So it is no wonder that exposed topsoil is easily washed away by rainstorms and flooding rivers or blown away by wind. Although dust storms are not uncommon in many parts of the world, the full extent of the terrifying damage that wind can do to dry and unprotected land was not fully realized until that fateful day, May 12, 1934, when the soil rose like a wall, and cataclysmic clouds of earth particles from the plains of Texas, Oklahoma, western Kansas, and eastern New Mexico darkened the sun from the Rocky Mountains to the Atlantic, carrying away enough topsoil to lay down a seven-inch blanket on 1,800,000 farms of 160 acres each.

The process of progressive removal of particles of topsoil, earth, or rock from the parent-mass through the steady action of water, wind, or ice is called erosion. Erosion can take many forms, but two basically different kinds must be distinguished: Sheet erosion and channel erosion.

Sheet erosion is the relatively uniform removal of soil in thin layers, a little at a time, spread more or less evenly over larger areas of ground. It was sheet erosion through the action of wind that devastated the Great Plains and created the "Dust Bowl." And it is primarily sheet erosion through the action of rain which destroys the blanket of topsoil on deforested land. Sheet erosion is often so insinuating that it is difficult to detect before it is too late: the sorting action of wind and water removes the finest particles first, and it is precisely these finest particles which are the most valuable biologically, the crumbs of decaying organic material, the grains of nutritiously important minerals—while the relatively worthless coarser sands and gravels are left behind.

Channel erosion is the cutting of clearly marked trenches by a concentrated flow of water. Channel erosion produces the familiar gullies cut into previously smooth hillsides and slopes, and the beds of valley-bottom streams that are permanent features of the landscape. The most magnificent product of channel erosion is the Grand Canyon.

Erosion is an aspect of nature that existed ever since the earth became sufficiently cool for steam to condense into water. It is a leveler of mountains and a carver of rivers. It was erosion that gave the massive face of the earth the features we see today. It is an irresistible force which, if left to its own devices, manifests itself normally in such a slow manner that plant growth and animal life can easily adjust to the gradual changes. But this process was altered when man became numerous and powerful enough to add his own destructiveness to that of nature. Believing himself created in the image of God, with god-like wisdom and power, he set out to subjugate the world, to remake and exploit it for his own purpose. Man took over the soil.

Everything went well as long as populations were relatively small. Although Thomas Malthus had with prophetic insight predicted as early as 1798 that the earth's population would eventually outgrow the earth's food supply, it took nearly another 200 years before more than a mere handful of people became aware of this threat. Up to that time, the general attitude was that we could always increase our food supply by wider application of scientific methods, discovery of new resources, and cultivation of additional acreage. Optimists kept reminding us that the Dutch, an industrious and prosperous people, managed to produce a good and varied diet on only two-thirds of an acre per person, implying that if their efficient methods were more generally used, enough food could be produced to feed some 30 billion people. Others went even further and, citing Japanese standards of agriculture and diet, held that the earth could support a population of 90 billion people. Still others never even questioned the issue, serene in their belief that Providence would provide.

Unfortunately, this kind of thinking is dangerous because it leads to a false sense of security. To begin with, large areas of the globe simply do not lend themselves to the kind of super-agriculture practiced in Holland and Japan. But still more serious is the fact that, no matter how much more food we may be able to produce, sooner or later we must arrive at a saturation point, for the very simple reason that the earth's surface is limited.

Figure it out for yourself: The total area of the globe is about 196,951,000 square miles. Of these, 70.6 per cent are covered by the sea. Of the remainder, more than one-third is uninhabitable, consisting of polar wastelands, rugged mountains, and waterless natural deserts. What is left are some 25,000,000 square miles or approximately 16 billion acres. Included in this figure, however, are forests, grasslands, and land occupied by cities and towns, industrial complexes, highways, railroad rights-of-ways, airfields, artillery and bombing ranges, nuclear testing sites (!), as well as large areas of land that have been ruined beyond reclamation through deforestation, overgrazing, or one-sided cultivation of unsuitable crops—the man-made deserts. Deducting all these from our figure of 16 billion acres, we are left with some 4 billion acres of potentially arable land. Even this figure may still be too high because, according to another survey made by the U.S. Department of State shortly before World War II, the total cultivated land area of the world at that time amounted to only $2^1/_2$ billion acres.

For the sake of argument, let's assume that the world contains $3^1/_2$ billion acres of arable land and $3^1/_2$ billion people, a number which, according to conservative projections, will be reached before 1970. This would amount to exactly one acre per capita. But according to generally accepted figures a minimum of $2^1/_2$ acres per capita is required to assure everybody of an adequate and healthy daily diet.

But let's try again and use the rock-bottom figure of one-tenth of an acre per capita in our calculation since, after all, this is the per capita figure for Japan. Using this cruelly low per capita average, we come to the conclusion that the world should be able to support a population of 35 billion people (not 90 billion, as the optimists would have us believe). However, these 35 billion people must also manage to occupy no more living space than our present population, since assigning additional acreage for housing, etc., would invalidate our calculations.

Everyone has heard of the "population explosion," but not everyone is fully aware of its implications. According to the best available estimates, during the middle of the seventeenth century the number of people in the entire world was between 500 and 550 million. By 1900, the figure had risen to 1,550 million. Sixty-two years later, it stood at 3,102 million. In other words, although man's ascent was slow in the beginning, the rate of population growth accelerated: It took hundreds of thousands of years before man's numbers reached a certain level—some 500 million; then, during the next two-hundred and fifty years, *the number of people tripled*. Then acceleration turned into explosion: within the unbelievably short span of only sixty-two years, *the world's population doubled*. At present, in the fall of 1966, the estimated number of people is 3,340 million and increasing more rapidly than ever—*at the rate of 170,000 more births than deaths per day!*

Projecting these statistics into the future, we find that the population of the world will double again within the next 40 years, quadruple within the next 70 years, and increase tenfold within the next 100 years. This means that for every man, woman, and child living today there will be ten men, ten woman, and ten children in the year 2066 for a total of some 34 billion people. In other words, taking into account the lowest possible per capita figure of one-tenth of an acre, *the ultimate number of people which the world could possibly carry will be reached within a hundred years.*

Moreover, these figures are only theoretical. In reality, the breaking point will arrive much sooner, since 1) our calculations assumed a near-starvation diet for all, and 2) a hundredfold increase in the number of people requires large additional areas for housing, industry, surface transportation, etc. (even if we think in terms of thousand-story skyscrapers), with corresponding reductions in land area available for the production of food.

These, then, are the facts we must face. The figures speak for themselves. They cannot be altered by any amount of juggling, nor by faith and prayer, nor by invocating Almighty God.

It should be obvious to anyone that humanity is headed toward disaster of totally unimaginable proportions unless preventive steps are taken immediately. Some people may believe that advances in food technology and synthesis; use of atomic power to transform mountains, deserts, and arctic wastelands so that they can be planted with crops; plus concentrated exploitation of the food resources of the sea, will make it possible to feed much larger numbers of people than we can visualize today. Perhaps, as a stop-gap; but for how long? For, as the population keeps increasing, sooner or later the day must come

when neither food nor space is left, for the simple reason that both food and space are limited whereas population is potentially unlimited. And even if population growth should stop accelerating and merely continue at its present rate, simple arithmetic shows that already by the year 2600 the number of human beings would be so great that there would be *one person to every square yard of land*.

Thus it must be obvious to all thinking people that there is only one way to avert a catastrophe which probably would mean the end of the human race: since we cannot increase the size of the earth, the only alternative is that we voluntarily restrict our numbers to an order of magnitude which is in harmony with existing means of subsistence.

No longer can we play the role of children who trust that a Heavenly Father will take care of us and tend to all our needs. Man must begin acting like a man, because he alone is answerable for the future of mankind.

The spiritual legacy of trees

During last summer's drive across the continent we passed through many towns, for the most part anonymous, stone-faced—typical American cities. But then we came to Mobile, Alabama. And weary as we were after the long, hard drive in the heat, we were refreshed. For here we were welcomed by trees. Double rows of live oaks lined the thoroughfares, their immense curving trunks and boughs rising high until they met in great arches—a triumphal avenue of green.

Much as we welcomed the physical relief—the contrast between the heat and glare of the open road and the soothing coolness of green shade—still stronger was a joyous sensation of having come home. It is not easy to describe the difference between physical and emotional relief except, perhaps, by analogy: entering an air-cooled building on a hot day one feels immediate physical relief; entering the cool dimness of a great cathedral—no matter whether believer or atheist—one feels something of what we experienced among the live oaks of Mobile.

Perhaps our feeling for trees is a heritage from very ancient times. How can one explain that young spiders know how to spin the intricate geometry of their webs or that an oriole knows how to construct its exquisitely complicated nest except by instinct? No parent ever taught these animals the necessary skills—they were inherited. So why could we not have inherited our love of trees?

Strong evidence for man's ancestral origin in the forest is the human hand. Although there are a few, such as the English anatomist F. Wood Jones, the late Henry Fairfield Osborn, and William L. Straus, Jr., of Johns Hopkins University, who take a somewhat more skeptical attitude, an impressive number of scientists have concluded that only an arboreal life could have led to the development of the human hand. In the tree-living primates the thumb is set apart from the other digits, opposable, making the hand a tool adapted to grasping. But grasping what? Certainly not food—for the precursors of these animals were already well equipped to "grasp" their food without the aid of hands. So what else is there to grasp except the branches of trees? Why should these descendants of the insectivores, adapted to running on the ground, have gradually changed into a totally different type of creature, an animal with mobile arms instead of forelegs and hands instead of paws, unless they derived some important advantage from this transformation, such as a better chance for survival in their new environment—the world of trees?

An arboreal life offers refuge from predators, shelter from the elements, a more equable climate, and an abundance of food. And life in the trees promotes physical agility, which in turn demands mental alertness, swiftness of reaction, and a sharp and observing eye, qualities which must be backed up by, or lead to the development of, a superior type of brain. Few of us have seen monkeys cavort and play in their natural environment, but all of us have watched them in the zoo displaying sure-footedness and distance-judging ability that borders on the fantastic. Is it then too much to assume that a primitive, tarsier-like creature with the agility and alertness of a squirrel, and forelimb joints that allow rotation of the bones, could through eons of time ultimately evolve into man?

Further supporting the hypothesis of man's origin in the forest is the prevalence of myths that deal with trees. This should not surprise anyone who ever spent a stormy night in the woods or watched the dawn rise over the forest. It is easy to imagine how these "dawnmen" must have felt when the night wind howled in the trees, lightning split the darkness with blinding bolts of light, and crashing thunder rolled and reverberated through the forest. To those halfmen who had already left the security of an instinct-ruled animal life, who stood on the threshold of conceptual thought, the mighty voices of the storm must have been conclusive evidence of the existence of powerful spirits. Shrieks and howls and groans are voices, and to frightened man it must have made no difference whether these voices issued from the throats of animals or the branches of wind-whipped, rain-lashed trees.

Thus it is not surprising—and surviving myths confirm this—that primitive man invested trees with a demonic life of their own, in a world populated with a fearful host of spirits and ogres, witches and gnomes, fairies, elves, and trolls. Pixies and leprechauns mischievously hid behind trees, nymphs and dryads danced among diaphanous dawn mists. Satyrs and fauns played their cruel jokes on the unwary traveler who had the misfortune to pass through haunted woods.

The fear of spooks and ghosts lives on. Considering the present state of enlightenment, this seems to indicate that such feelings are so deeply rooted in our subconscious minds that they can be explained only on the basis of inherited instincts. One such dread dating from the beginning of consciousness may be the fear of darkness—a memory haunting us ever since man had to live through starless forest nights. Walking in the woods at night even relatively sophisticated people have been known to succumb to this fear, imagining all kinds of unholy apparitions. By the pale light of a waning moon the bole of a broken tree assumes the form of a witch, its last remaining branch a shriveled arm beckoning with bony finger. A humped, crouching shape where the shadows are deepest is not a moss-covered stump but a silent watching gnome. A pale luminescence emanating from beneath a rotting log, actually the fluorescence of fungi, is a ghostly light guarding buried treasure. Pale wreaths of mist rising from marshy grounds are elves dancing by moonlight. All around the silent forest unseen eyes stare out of inky darkness. Images hoary with age are remembered—long-forgotten terrors.

Panic grips one, the very name of this fear a reminder of ancient Pan whose sudden appearance allegedly evoked this uncontrollable dread.

The world-wide veneration of trees in ancient times is documented by the rich legacy of surviving legends from virtually every part of the earth, and the corroborating evidence of the tree cults of present-day aborigines. This is a fascinating subject which has been admirably treated by Sir James George Frazer in *The Golden Bough*.

During Roman times most of Europe was still blanketed by vast primeval forests which, in Caesar's time, covered the land from the Rhine eastward for a distance "greater than a man could travel in two months." Here the Germans worshiped their gods in sacred groves, and the intensity of their veneration of trees can be measured by the terrible punishment that awaited anyone who broke the law that forbade stripping the bark of a living tree: first, his navel was cut out and spiked to the injured tree; then, the culprit was driven in circles around the trunk until the full length of his gut was wound around the tree. The symbolism which underlies this ritual is, of course, the same as that which underlies the ancient Hebrew doctrine of "an eye for an eye"—the murderer's life for the life of the murdered tree. It must have seemed only fitting that the wound inflicted on the body of the tree should be dressed with substance from the body of the culprit. I cannot help thinking of this ghastly form of justice every time I see a lovely white birch which vandals have defiled by peeling off strips of bark.

Because they were holy, sacred groves, like churches during the Middle Ages, were sanctuaries where political fugitives and common criminals could find asylum; the boundaries of the grove were inviolable. Groves also were places where the deity revealed itself and, in the form of oracles, made pronouncements about the future. Famous in its time was the sacred grove near Upsala, the ancient religious center of Sweden; every one of its numerous trees was venerated as holy. Even the Bible repeatedly contains references to sacred groves, although here they were considered blasphemous vestiges of idolatry that had to be dealt with accordingly: "But ye shall destroy their altars, break their images, and cut down their groves" (Exodus 34:13). Unfortunately, modern missionaries, perpetuating ancient dogmas with heavy-handed literalness, have seen fit to follow this example all over the world with the result that a great many of these sacred groves are now destroyed. Such misguided zeal is all the more deplorable since these groves were often the only preserved remains of ancient forests, containing specimens of plants and trees otherwise extremely rare or extinct. One such tree, for example, is the ginkgo, no longer existent in the wild state; it was saved from extinction only because it was venerated in ancient China and cultivated in sacred temple groves.

But in spite of this deliberate destruction, sacred groves still exist in many of the more primitive countries; a number of interesting references to such groves are given in *Man's Role in Changing the Face of the Earth*, edited by William L. Thomas, Jr., and others. Here are a few examples: On the islands of Borneo and Timor, botanists were not permitted to collect plant material because the places where the most interesting specimens could be found were holy. In India a number of sacred groves were reported in areas inhabited by primitive tribes. Another sacred grove was found on Luzon in the Philippines. The only temples of the Mundas of Chota Nagpur are their village *sarnas*, their sacred groves. In Sumatra, the Pardembanan Batak held places sacred where the lateral growth of exposed tree roots covered by fallen leaves had made a roof over a little forest stream; listening to the gentle murmur of the water filled these people with reverence, and they could not be persuaded to clear such places for the establishment of plantations. And the Dairi Batak had sacred groves in which one particular tree was revered as the seat of the deity to which they addressed their prayers. From equatorial Africa, too, numerous sacred groves have been reported still in use as places of worship all along a belt that stretches from Mozambique on the eastern shore to the Ivory Coast in the west.

Individual trees have likewise been held sacred from time immemorial. Famous from Norse mythology is the great ash Yggdrasill, the World Tree, Tree of the Universe, Tree of Existence and Life. Rooted deep down in the Underworld, in Hel, the kingdom of death, its boughs span the universe and its crown touches the very heights of heaven. At its foot, where its roots are watered by the Sacred Well, eternally sit the three Fates, the Nornir, divine giantesses who determine the course of human life.

In Europe, the most highly venerated tree was the oak. The reason for this is easy to see: oaks are the by far most impressive of all European trees (see picture pages 17 and 158–159). Another, and perhaps deeper and more significant, explanation is that oaks are more often struck by lightning than any other European tree. Why this is so is still not known, but there can be no doubt that this phenomenon was already familiar to primitive man. Clearly, a tree that more often than any other received the sacred fire of heaven was special, the favorite of the gods, perhaps even the seat of the deity himself, who during a thunderstorm descended to earth in the form of a blinding flash. Then, too, there is the importance of fire for man. Without our modern conveniences for producing fire, it was difficult to come by. And prior to the discovery that fire could be kindled by friction —by rubbing two pieces of dry wood rapidly together—the only way to possess fire was to steal it, in Promethean fashion, from a lightning-ignited burning tree. Standing in the presence of such a smoldering tree, those early men doubtlessly felt something of the same awe that gripped Moses in the presence of the burning bush: a miracle had happened, the deity had visited the earth and made man the gift of fire. Fire may even have been conceived of as a property of the tree itself from which it could be extracted like sap. Corroboration for this hypothesis can be found in the legends of the Californian Indians of the Maidu and Senal tribes that the world originally was a mass of fire which gradually withdrew to the interior; from there it passed through the roots into the trunks and branches of trees from which it can be extracted with fire drills.

Does it still seem strange that our ancestors believed the great trunks of lightning-blasted, fire-blackened oaks were holy?

Later, when people no longer believed that trees were gods but only symbols of the deity, the oak became the symbol of the thundergod. Thus, in Teutonic mythology the oak was the sacred tree of Donar, Thunar, or Thor, wielder of the hammer, god of lightning and thunder. Similarly, the ancient Greeks and Romans venerated the oak as the symbol of their thundergods, Zeus and Jupiter. One of the most famous sanctuaries in ancient Greece was the sacred grove of Dodona where the voice of mighty Zeus could be heard in the rustling leaves of an oracular oak. During imperial times a victorious Roman general returned in triumphal procession, a wreath of laurel encircling his brow, while over his head a slave held a massive crown of oak leaves fashioned of gold.

Other peoples and civilizations worshiped other trees. In Asia Buddhists held the fig tree sacred, and not for nothing is the Latin name of the pipal *Ficus religiosa* (that a great fig tree can inspire religious feelings should be evident from picture pages 108–109). An Indian tree, the Karm *(Nauclea parvifolia)*, venerated by the Oraon and Kharwar tribes of Chota Nagpur, was spared even when all other trees were cut down to make way for plantations. That the ginkgo escaped oblivion only because it was held sacred has already been mentioned. And Livingstone reported from Africa in 1875 that a tree which the natives venerated under the name "bokonto" could only be found in sacred groves near Tamiala in what today is Nyasaland, but was exterminated everywhere else.

Further indications of the power which trees held over the lives and minds of people everywhere is the constant recurrence of tree images of a more general kind. The Bible, for example, speaks of the Tree of Knowledge—the forbidden tree whose fruit must not be tasted lest man lose his innocence. The Persians had their Tree of Immortality, the Aryans their World Tree Yggdrasill, the Buddhists their Tree of Enlightenment, the Moslems their Tree of Hospitality, and the Jews their Tree of Temptation.

With the ascent of Christianity, tree worship became sublimated, or degenerated into superstition as missionaries went out on their global crusades. But so persistent is the power of old traditions that vestiges of ancient tree cults can still be found even among modern civilized people. In many European countries, on the eve of St. John's Day, June 23, young people still dance around the May poles in celebration of Midsummer Day, the summer solstice, the great turning point of the seasons when the sun begins its long downward climb along the heavenly road. And on *Walborgsmässafton*, the evening of April 30, huge bonfires still blaze on countless hills and knolls in Sweden in celebration of the arrival of spring while the fiddles play and the young folks dance around in a ring. A thousand years of persuasive efforts by the Church have not extirpated these ancient customs, remnants of bygone days when man

31

still lived in harmony with nature and trees were venerated as gods.

Among the superstitions that originate in ancient tree cults are the widespread belief that it brings luck to dance and kiss under the mistletoe and the custom of hanging a wreath of holly on the door at Christmas time. Both traditions allegedly date back to the days of the Druids who, as legend has it, placed these evergreens on their altars in winter to give a home to the elves while the trees were bare. Likewise, the particular significance of the olive branch as a symbol of peace and forgiveness, the laurel as a symbol of honor and accomplishment, and even the crown of thorns as a symbol of suffering mankind have roots that are far older than the conscious memory of man. Even our custom of taking home a spruce or fir for Christmas and decorating it gaily with glitter and lights has been traced back to the World Tree Yggdrasill and the stars that once blazed in its heaven-like crown. And it was only a little more than thirty years ago that I myself photographed a tree in Sweden which, according to ancient legend and the local peasantry, had the power to cure sickness in children. The naked child was dragged through an opening formed by the exposed roots and the earth on a Thursday night and would then recover. This ceremony, *smöja* (*smyga*—sneak), is based on the belief that a kind of rebirth of the child occurs when he is passed through the port formed on one side by the soil (representing the Earth Goddess) and on the other by the roots of the magic-endowed tree. That this treatment is considered most effective when performed on a Thursday is, of course, because Thursday (*torsdag* in Swedish) is the day of Thor, the Aryan thundergod.

Thus it is obvious that remnants of ancient tree cults still cast their spells today. And although some of these tree-cult-inspired customs are no more than superstitions, useless and even injurious, others are charming and beautiful. What would Christmas be without a tree? Where is the hero who would refuse the laurel wreath? Or the couple who does not enjoy the privileges offered by the mistletoe? One of the seasonal pleasures in many city dwellers' lives is passing the Christmas trees standing in rows along the curb in December and smelling their resinous fragrance, a greeting from faraway woods. And one of my more persistent memories from adolescence, when I worked as an apprentice in a cabinetmaker's shop, is the clean sweet smell of pine wood and the acrid, exciting odor of oak. I still cannot pass a lumberyard or see plywood being loaded on a truck without pausing and breathing deeply, and I am not sure whether the pleasure I feel is due to associations with days spent in the woods or a manifestation of those much older memories that are part of our evolutionary inheritance.

Again I am sitting at the edge of the woods, but now the color of my world has changed. Autumn is here and the trees are ablaze with many colors—the burgundy of the dogwood, its branches now tipped with clusters of scarlet drupes; the rich old gold of tulip tree and hickory; the bright clean yellow of sugar maple and birch; the mauve and tarnished bronze of ash; the burning reds and oranges of red maple, sumach, and sassafras; the somber greens, browns, and purples of oaks.

I try to understand the message of the trees by giving my thoughts free rein. I feel great patience and tenacity, humility and acceptance of the inevitable—qualities that well befit proud man. I think about the purpose of all life and ask myself: What is the purpose of a tree? What is the purpose of an animal? What is the purpose of man? And it occurs to me that perhaps the purpose of all living things is simply living—to play our nature-assigned role in the great drama of life; to participate, be it on ever so modest a scale, in the orderly unfolding of the cosmos. Unknowingly, if a tree; instinctively, if an animal; with full awareness, if man. To take what we need, but no more. To know that we exist on borrowed substance. And, when the time we are given has run out, to return this substance to the great treasury of the earth so that other living things may use it again and, in using it, pass on that mysterious force we call life. To be of open mind and free of prejudice, feeling, though human, related to the animals and plants, a cog in the machinery of the universe, a humble yet vital part, privileged to wield immense power, yet honor-bound to respect the rights of other living things. And, above all, to treasure the gift of life.

II
Some Facts about Trees

Everyone knows what a tree is. But a difference exists between popular and scientific definitions of a tree. According to popular concepts, for example, oaks, maples, Joshua trees, pines, and coconut palms are all trees; according to the more precise botanical meaning of the term, however, only oaks, maples, and pines qualify as trees, whereas the Joshuas and coconut palms are merely plants—the first a member of the lily family *(Liliaceae)* and the latter a member of the palm family *(Palmae)*. They fail to qualify as trees because their trunks do not consist of wood, for, according to scientific definition, a tree is a *woody* plant with a *single stem* called a *trunk* that is *perennial*, i.e., that does not die after flowering only once. If a woody plant has several stems growing out of the same root it is usually called a "shrub." Unfortunately, this distinction between trees and shrubs is not infallible because certain kinds of trees—willows, birches, etc.—may have several trunks growing out of the same root system, yet because of their size not be classified as shrubs. Nonwoody plants are called *herbaceous* plants or herbs.

The difference between woody and nonwoody plants is the result of dissimilarities in the construction of their stem cells. The stem cell walls of woody plants are reinforced with a complex organic compound called "lignin," which is hard and therefore acts as a stiffener; nonwoody plants contain little or no lignin. This explains why woody plants stay erect even after the onset of frost, whereas most nonwoody plants wilt and collapse, although their roots may survive the winter and sprout again the following spring.

This book contains photographs and descriptions of several plants that are not trees in the strict botanical sense of the term. These are the traveler's-tree and yucca, the screw pine, palm, banana, and saguaro. I included these tree-like nontrees because they are unusual-looking plants that are common enough to be of interest to many people.

The dimensions of trees

Trees vary enormously in size. Those that venture as far north as the arctic tundra may struggle on for years and never grow more than knee-high; others, such as the redwood and Australian eucalyptus, rise more than 350 feet into the sky. Furthermore, a tree fortunate enough to germinate in rich river bottom land will, of course, grow faster and become bigger and taller than the same kind of tree rooted in a location where water is less plentiful.

The height and trunk diameter of a tree are therefore rather unreliable indicators of its age. As will be shown later when we come to the bristlecone pines (Chapter IV, picture pages 32–36), a thousand-year-old tree may be fewer than ten feet high; on the other hand, under favorable conditions, some of the fastest-growing trees may reach a height of fifty feet within ten years. The following list gives the dimensions of the largest known specimens of forty of the more common North American trees. It is based on the sixth (May 1966) edition of The American Forestry Association's *Social Register of Big Trees*, compiled by Kenneth B. Pomeroy and Dorothy Dixon, which records the measurements of a total of 385 different American trees.

Tree species	Height	Circumference at $4^1/_4$ feet	Spread	Location
Ailanthus	80′	18′8″	75′	Head of Harbor, New York
Ash, white	80′	22′3″	82′	Glenn Mills, Pennsylvania
Bald cypress	122′	39′8″	47′	Near Sharon, Tennessee
Beech, American	91′	18′5″	96′	Saugatuck, Michigan
Birch, paper	96′	10′11″	93′	Lake Leelanau, Michigan
Butternut	85′	11′9″	92′	St. Joseph County, Michigan
Catalpa, northern	93′	17′4″	74′	Lansing, Michigan

Tree species	Height	Circumference at $4\frac{1}{4}$ feet	Spread	Location
Cedar, incense	225′	16′3″	—	Umpqua National Forest, Oregon
Chestnut, American	90′	15′8″	64′	Oregon City, Oregon
Cottonwood, eastern	131′	25′9″	129′	Wayne, Michigan
Douglas fir, coast	221′	45′5″	61′	Olympic Nat'l Park, Washington
Elm, American	160′	24′7″	147′	Near Trigonia, Tennessee
Fir, balsam	116′	7′	33′	Porcupine Mts., Michigan
Hemlock, eastern	98′	19′9″	69′	Great Smoky Mts. Nat'l Park
Hickory, shagbark	100′	11′5″	113′	Chevy Chase, Maryland
Joshua tree	32′	12′6″	37′	Joshua Tree Nat'l Monument
Locust, black	85′	15′11″	60′	Near Jefferson, Indiana
Maple, red	136′	15′4″	95′	Near Utica, Michigan
Maple, sugar	116′	19′9″	75′	Garrett County, Maryland
Oak, black	125′	22′3″	85′	Warrensville Hgts., Ohio
Oak, live	78′	35′	168′	Near Hahnville, Louisiana
Oak, California live	108′	24′10″	129′	Chiles Va Mey, California
Oak, northern red	78′	26′4″	104′	Ashford, Connecticut
Oak, white	95′	27′8″	165′	Wye Mills, Maryland
Pine, bristlecone	40′	37′7″	45′	Inyo Nat'l Forest, California
Pine, eastern white	151′	17′11″	48′	Brule River State Forest, Wisconsin
Pine, ponderosa	246′	14′11″	—	Siskiyou Nat'l Forest, Oregon
Pine, sugar	170′	31′2″	56′	Stabislaus Nat'l Forest, California
Pine, western white	219′	21′3″	36′	Near Elk River, Idaho
Poplar, balsam	89′	11′11″	78′	Dawes Arboretum, Newark, Ohio
Redwood	368′	44′	—	Redwood Creek, California
Royal palm	100′	4′9″	12′	Collier Seminole State Park, Florida
Sequoia	272′	83′11″	90′	"General Sherman", Sequoia Nat'l Park, California
Spruce, Engelmann	140′	20′7″	34′	Williamette Nat'l Forest, Oregon
Sycamore, American	80′	32′10″	102′	Near South Bloomfield, Ohio
Sycamore, California	116′	27′	158′	Near Santa Barbara, California
Tulip tree	110′	24′3″	119′	Amelia, Virginia
Walnut, black	108′	20′3″	128′	Anne Arundel Cnty., Maryland
Willow, black	85′	26′1″	79′	Traverse City, Michigan
Willow, weeping	95′	19′7″	93′	Beverly Hills, Michigan

The highest tree in the world is an only recently discovered 368-foot tall redwood *(Sequoia sempervirens)* standing in Redwood Grove on the east bank of Redwood Creek in Humboldt County, northern California. Another redwood, named the "Founders' Tree" in honor of Dr. John C. Merriam, Madison Grant, and Dr. Henry Fairfield Osborn, founders of the "Save-the-Redwoods League," is 364 feet tall; it stands in the Founders' Grove of the Humboldt Redwoods State Park near Dyersville in northern California.

Although much more massive, sequoias are not so tall as redwoods. Here are the heights of five famous trees: McKinley Tree, 291 feet; Hart Tree, 278 feet; General Sherman Tree, 272 feet; Bole Tree, 269 feet; General Grant Tree, 267 feet. The fabulous dimensions of the Australian eucalyptus trees *(Eucalyptus regnans)*, which have allegedly reached heights of 464 and 435 feet (two trees which were felled in 1868 and 1872, respectively), are unconfirmed and are now believed to have been exaggerated.

The tree with the most massive trunk is the Montezuma cypress *(Taxodium mucronatum)* that stands in the churchyard in the village of Santa Maria del Tule near Oaxaca, Mexico. Its trunk has a circumference of 160 feet and a diameter of more than 50 feet, and requires the outstretched arms of twenty-seven men to span. Unfortunately, this tree has never been thoroughly studied by scientists, but some botanists believe that its enormous trunk actually consists of several individual trunks that gradually grew together. It is usually estimated to be between 3,000 and 5,000 years old, but this has never been established by actual ring count. According to a report in the *National Geographic Magazine* by Dr. Edmund

Schulman, who examined a wind-fallen branch, the tree in Tule probably has lived less than 1,500 years.

The oldest trees, and also the oldest living things on earth, are the bristlecone pines (*Pinus aristata,* see Chapter IV and picture pages 32–36). A living tree more than 4,600 years old by actual growth-ring count has been found; it germinated approximately 2,640 years before the birth of Christ. In addition, sixteen other specimens have been established by ring count as more than 4,000 years old. How growth rings can be counted without destroying the tree is explained in Chapter XIII.

Sequoias *(Sequoia gigantea)*—see picture pages 97–101 —although ever so much bigger and more impressive than bristlecone pines, do not seem to reach the fabulous age of the latter; the record age for sequoias is 3,212 years by ring count, established by a tree that was felled in 1892. However, this sequoia, which started growing in 1320 B.C. is surpassed in trunk diameter by several trees that are still standing and, therefore, may be older.
Less spectacular are the life spans of our more common trees. Maples and elms, for example, rarely exceed 300 years, oaks 500 years, and Douglas firs and western junipers 700 to 800 years.

"Oldest" of all trees, in the sense that as a kind or species it has existed for the longest period of time without changing—a veritable "living fossil"—is the ginkgo (*Ginkgo biloba,* see picture pages 30 and 37), which dates back to the Jurassic era, some 150 million years ago.

The fastest-growing tree is an Australian eucalyptus (*Eucalyptus saligna*) which has been reported to grow up to forty-five feet within two years.

The slowest-growing trees are those which have to survive under the extreme climatic conditions of drought, heat, and cold such as might be found in the desert, in the arctic, or on high mountains. Dr. Schulman found a bristlecone pine growing in California's Inyo National Forest at an altitude of 11,300 feet that was only three feet high, with a trunk three inches in diameter, yet was 700 years old by growth-ring count. And from a location near the

arctic tree line, a Sitka spruce has been reported that was only eleven inches high, with a trunk diameter of less than one inch; yet it was ninety-eight years old.

Eight hundred and sixty-five different species of trees, according to a report by the American Forestry Association, are found in the wild state in the continental United States. This number includes a few imports that have become acclimatized to such an extent that they now are able to reproduce themselves in the wild state without human assistance. This figure is almost four times as large as the total of all European trees, but it is only a fraction of the different species found in the humid tropics.

The names of trees

Being able to call a person by name immediately establishes a new relationship—less impersonal, friendlier, more enjoyable. This also applies to trees: a tree that we know by name becomes a friend that we recognize on sight and greet with pleasure. Learning to know trees by name is the first step to enjoying them.
Trees, like most plants and animals, have two kinds of name: popular and scientific. Maple, oak, and birch, for example, are popular names. Actually, these are generic names; they apply to certain groups of trees—the maples, the oaks, the birches—each of which contains several different kinds or *species*—sugar maple, red maple, Norway maple, etc.; white oak, pin oak, live oak, etc.; sweet birch, paper birch, gray birch, etc. However, popular names, each of which ideally should apply to only one specific kind of tree, have certain disadvantages which make them unsuitable for scientific purposes. They differ with different languages and are therefore not internationally understood. Their meaning is often unclear even to those who speak the language, because it is quite common for the same name to apply to two or more different kinds of tree (in English, for example, the name "ironwood" is used interchangeably for two different species of tree, *Carpinus caroliniana* and *Ostrya virginiana,* and "black willow" is the popular name of at least seven different species of *Salix*

(willow). Conversely, the same species of tree (or plant or animal) is often known by several different popular names, depending on where it is found. For example, the sycamore is also called "plane tree" and "buttonwood"; the tulip tree is also known as "yellow poplar"; the sweet birch also goes under the names "black birch" and "cherry birch."

To avoid confusion, scientists from all over the world have long since agreed to call each species of tree by a single Latin name. This has several advantages. Latin is a "dead" language, and therefore no longer subject to change. It is intelligible to scientific investigators all over the world, no matter what their native language. And it provides unambiguous identification even for those plants and animals (and there are tens of thousands) that have no popular names.

The Latin name of every plant and animal consists of two words (occasionally three) and an abbreviation. The scientific name of the sweet birch, for example, is *Betula lenta* L. The first word (which is always capitalized), *Betula*, is the name of the *genus* (or group of closely related species) to which the tree belongs, in this case the birches. The second word (which is usually descriptive) designates the particular kind (or *species*) of plant or animal. Therefore, if we talk about *Betula lenta* L., it means that we have a sweet birch in mind and not, for example, a paper birch or a gray birch. Finally, the abbreviation indicates the name of the scientist who was the first to describe the particular species, in this case Linnaeus, the Swedish botanist who is also known as the "father of systematic botany."

An important advantage of this system of classification is that, like a chemical formula, it already contains a certain amount of information about the respective tree. For example, all maple trees belong to the genus *Acer*, and, consequently, the Latin names of all the different species of maple begin with that word. By contrast, the popular names of the different species of maple often give no such indication. For although we speak of sugar maple, red maple, Norway maple, etc., some other members of the genus *Acer* have such popular names as black ash, moosewood, buckwood, and box elder—names which certainly do not imply that each of these trees is actually a maple.

Species and *genera* (plural of *genus*) are subdivisions of an elaborate and precise system of classification which places every single kind of tree (or plant or animal) in clear relationship to all the others. The smallest unit of this system is the *species*—each species name designates only one single, specific kind of tree. The next larger unit is the *genus*—all closely related species belong to the same genus. In similar fashion, related genera are grouped together as a *family* and related families as an *order*. Related orders, in turn, are grouped together in a *class*, and related classes in a *division*. Finally, a number of divisions constitute a *kingdom*.

A very brief history of trees

Trees are plants, and plants, like animals, originated in the sea. Precisely when this momentous event took place is not known, but it is certain that it was more than 2,000 million years ago.

This awesome figure is not a figment of the imagination, but based on concrete evidence—fossils and rocks. Fossils are the preserved remains or traces of animals or plants of past geological ages that have been dug out of the earth or found imbedded in rocks. These are studied by paleontologists—scientists who study the life of the past—or, in the case of plants, by paleobotanists—botanists specializing in ancient plant life—who, in cooperation with geologists and experts in other fields, have been able to date these remains by a number of methods, the most ingenious and accurate of which is based on the chemical breakdown of uranium to lead and helium. The rate at which this conversion proceeds is known, and, since this rate is not affected by ordinary changes in temperature or pressure, the age of almost any rock sample can be determined by establishing the proportions of its uranium and lead content. Although these elements are usually present in only minute quantities, modern methods of microchemistry are so incredibly sensitive that it has been possible to assign surprisingly definite dates to the different rock strata which comprise the crust of the earth and to arrive at a "calendar of events" which, in simplified form, is shown in the following chart.

Era	Period	Important plants and animals	Years ago
Cenozoic (recent life)	Quarternary	Age of herbaceous flowering plants and man.	2 million
	Tertiary	Age of *Angiosperms* and higher mammals.	75 million
Mesozoic (middle life)	Cretaceous	Rise of *Angiosperms*. Greatest development of cycads. Decline of conifers, ferns, and other Jurassic plants. Decline of giant reptiles, further evolution of mammals.	135 million
	Jurassic	Greatest development of ginkgoales, conifers, horsetails. Giant dinosaurs; first birds.	165 million
	Triassic	Disappearance of many ancient plant forms. First appearance of modern plant types. Conifer forests. Rise of ginkoales. Decline of seed ferns. Early dinosaurs and primitive mammals.	200 million
Paleozoic (old life)	Permian	Decline of carboniferous plants. Rise of reptiles.	230 million
	Carboniferous	Formation of major coal beds. Ferns and seed ferns, sigillaria, lepidodendron, ancient conifers, liverworts and mosses. Giant insects. Spread of amphibia.	300 million
	Devonian	Evolution of advanced types of plant structures. Early ferns, lepidodendrons, and *Gymnosperms*. First amphibia. Rise of marine fish.	350 million
	Silurian	First vascular land plants.	400 million
	Ordovician Cambrian	Calcareous algae. Earliest aquatic vertebrates. All invertebrate phyla.	600 million
Proterozoic (earlier life)	Pre-Cambrian	Algae and bacteria. Few fossils.	2,000 million
Archeozoic (ancient life)		Only indirect evidence of life.	3,000 million

According to fossil evidence, the first known plants were bluegreen algae (although others, still more primitive, must have existed before them, but so far no direct vestiges of these have been discovered); their traces were found in Canadian rocks that had been deposited some 2,000 million years ago. These algae, which presumably flourished in warm and shallow seas, proliferated, changed, branched out, and split into new forms which in turn evolved. They are the ur-ancestors of all modern plants.

Because the fossil evidence, particularly in regard to the earliest plants, is extremely sketchy, it is not known exactly how this evolution occurred and, in particular, which branch of a lower group of plants changed sufficiently to give rise to the next higher group. But although paleobotanists as yet have not been able to show precisely how this rise from algae to flowering plants took place, they have discovered a number of definite steps in the ladder of plant evolution. Each step represents a momentous advance over the previous one, the entire sequence culminating in our present flowering plants. Here is a synopsis, the evolution of plant life on earth: *The first organized living organisms*—neither animal nor plant yet the precursors of both—were the archaic bacteria of the Pre-Cambrian period which came into being more than 2,000 million years ago. The main difference between these and our modern bacteria is that early bacteria must have been able to synthesize food from inorganic substances (since organic substances did not exist as yet), whereas modern bacteria are either parasites or saprophytes (consumers of dead organic matter). Bacteria are among the smallest of all living things, measuring from one-half to four microns—and a micron, the symbol of which is the Greek letter mu (μ), is only $1/1000$ mm or approximately $1/25,000$ of an inch. Yet, in spite of their "microscopic size," they are highly organized, complex organisms, far from the "blob of animated matter" many people assume them to be.

The first plants able to produce oxygen were the already mentioned bluegreen algae, the "ur-algae" of the Pre-Cambrian period, of which very little is known. They flourished some 2 billion years ago.

37

The first plants to produce food by photosynthesis—i.e., able to utilize the energy of the sun (as is explained in Chapter IX)—were the *Chlorophyta*, which appeared some 600 million years ago, during the Cambrian period. They were the ancestors of our modern green and brown algae, dinoflagellates, liverworts, and mosses.

The first plants to possess true stems were the *Psilopsidae*, simple vascular plants (possessors of a conductive system); only four species representing this archaic type are still living today. They first appeared approximately 420 million years ago, during the Silurian period, and are the progenitors of our club mosses and horsetails.

The first plants to evolve true leaves—the *Filicophyta*—date back some 390 million years to the Devonian period. They are the ancestors of our modern ferns.

The first plants to produce true seeds—the *Gymnosperms*—made their appearance approximately 345 million years ago during the Carboniferous period. The only surviving representatives of this class are ninety species of cycads (plants that somewhat resemble palms), seventy species of *Gnetales* (shrubby or vine-like plants), 550 species of conifers (our "softwoods" or "evergreens"), and the ginkgo.

The first plants to bear true flowers were the *Angiosperms*, which appeared some 135 million years ago during the Cretaceous period. They are the most successful of all plant types, and, of a total of some 350,000 known plants living today (which includes all types from bacteria on up), more than 200,000 belong to this flowering class. *Angiosperms* are divided into two sub-classes: the *Monocotyledons*, most of which can be recognized easily by their leaves, which have parallel veins (like our grasses, orchids, yuccas, or palms), and the *Dicotyledons*, which generally possess netted-veined leaves (like our maples or oaks).

The first tree-like plants appeared during the Devonian period, some 400 million years ago. They reached their climax during the Carboniferous period, when the world's climate was uniformly warm and water abundant. Favorable growing conditions produced immense forest swamps—squelchy bogs choked with dead vegetation and fallen trees dominated by two kinds of plant which no longer exist except in miniature: our club mosses and horsetails. Although probably not directly descended from those ancient plants, they resemble them sufficiently in general appearance so that, with a bit of discomfort and some imagination, one can get a fair idea of how a Carboniferous swamp jungle may have looked by lying down among the horsetails and club mosses, bringing one's eye close to the ground, looking up into their tiny crowns, and visualizing this miniature forest enlarged a hundred-fold. What only a moment ago was a tiny scale-stemmed plant called a "club moss" is now a huge *Lepidodendron* or *Sigillaria* tree, its massive three-foot-wide trunk rising more than one hundred feet into the steamy jungle air. Leaf scars give its bark the scaly appearance of reptile hide, as if to foreshadow the saurians who 100 million years later were to rule the world. *Calamites* resembling grotesquely overgrown horsetails tower forty to fifty feet, their stiff, spiky branches arranged in tiers of whorls around their jointed, ridged stems, their trunks more than a foot in diameter. But not a single flower lends color to this endless monotony of unrelieved green, where giant roaches scuttle through the piles of plant debris that litter the ground while *Meganeura*, immense dragonfly-like insects with wing spans of two-and-a-half feet, cruise over black swamp water.

An eery silence fills these ancient forests in which no higher animals yet exist. No birds sing or call; no animals cry out in joy or fear or pain. Even the air, stagnant and fetid with decay, bears little resemblance to the air we breathe today, because it is still heavy with an overabundance of poisonous carbon gas lethal to any modern animal or man.

It is mainly due to the plants of the Carboniferous swamp forests which, in order to build their tissues, absorbed immense amounts of carbon from the atmosphere—carbon which later was to become coal—that our air is fit for man to breathe. And it is ironic that now man, by burning enormous quantities of coal, in turn gives back to the air this very carbon, poisoning the atmosphere in detriment to his health and life.

Such were the Carboniferous swamps that flourished for 100 million years, generation after generation of plants rising and maturing and subsiding in decay in endless succession, layer piling on layer, partly rotting at the bottom, growing at the top, producing unimaginable amounts of vegetable matter. From time to time devastating floods inundated these forests, drowning the vegetation and burying it under layers of silt. And again the land emerged and rose, and new forests grew and flourished for half a million years, sank below the surface of flooding waters, and were once more buried in mud and silt. This cycle repeated itself over and over again. And gradually, in a process that went on through eons, these ancient forests, choked off by sediment and protected from normal decay by the exclusion of air, turned under the unimaginable pressure of overlaying mountains into coal.

The immensity of the Carboniferous forests can be measured by the fact that the largest American coal bed extends continuously through parts of Montana and Wyoming into the Dakotas and that the Pittsburgh field, although smaller, nevertheless covers some 12,000 square miles. In West Virginia, Nova Scotia, and Germany successions of more than one hundred individual coal seams, separated by layers of rock, have been found piled on top of one another, representing the graveyards of more than a hundred different swamps. Some coal seams are only a few inches thick, others several hundred feet. The average thickness of a workable coal seam was once three to four feet, but nowadays, with coal becoming scarcer, considerably thinner seams are worked profitably with automatic machines. The thickest coal bed so far discovered is in China. It is over 400 feet thick, and it has been calculated that the original accumulation of vegetable matter must have exceeded 8,000 feet. Since coal is produced at an average rate of $1\frac{1}{2}$ inches per thousand years, this tremendous coal bed is proof that a Carboniferous swamp forest flourished there uninterruptedly for over three million years.

During the Permian period world-wide climatic and geophysical changes produced long cold, dry periods, which led to the extensive formation of both glaciers and deserts which culminated in the ice age. This brought an end to the Carboniferous swamp forest and its scaly trees. Although a few of its members were able to adapt to the new conditions to evolve, during the next 200 million years, into the horsetails, club mosses, and ferns of today, the others succumbed and became extinct.

During the Mesozoic era the dominant land plants were *Gymnosperms*—cycads, *Bennettitales*, and conifers. The cycads were palm-like plants, which managed to survive and are represented today by ninety living species. The now extinct order *Bennettitales* consisted of coarse, thickset plants with heavy stems bearing a crown of palm-like leaves. The conifers were mostly large trees. The enormous trunks of one species, *Auricarioxylon arizonicum*, a distant relative of our monkeypuzzle tree and the Norfolk Island pine, can still be seen in petrified form in the Petrified Forest National Monument in Arizona, transformed into silica and colorful agate.

The *Gymnosperms*—the "naked-seed plants"—reached their climax during the Jurassic period some 165 million years ago and then went into a decline, giving way to the *Angiosperms*—the "encased-seed plants"—with a superior method of propagation. Today, fewer than 700 species of *Gymnosperms* survive. Of these, 550 are conifers, our "softwoods" or "evergreens"—the redwoods and sequoias; pines and larches; hemlock, spruce, and fir; the cypresses, cedars, and junipers. In addition, there is that strange relic, that "living fossil" that dates back to Permian times, the tree beloved by our big-city park commissioners because it is relatively resistant to automobile exhaust fumes: the maidenhair tree, or ginkgo. Together with ninety living species of cycads and seventy of *Gnetales*, this is all that remains of the once mighty empire of the *Gymnosperms*. The Cenozoic era—which dates from approximately 75 million years—is the age of the *Angiosperms*, the "encased-seed plants," which includes all our modern trees and tree-like plants with the exception of the conifers, the cycads, and the ginkgo: e.g., the oaks and elms, birches and beeches, apple trees and rubber trees, and hundreds of others, and the tree-like nontrees such as palms, yuccas, and saguaros. *Angiosperms* form the northern hardwood forests that cover large parts of the United States, Canada, and Europe. They are the trees of the tropical rain forests—rubber and fig, polisander, mahogany, banyan, ebony, and all the others that comprise the immense jungles of the Amazon and the Congo, of India, Malaysia, and the Philippines. They are the new rulers of the forest.

Picture pages 1–16

1. Douglas fir *(Pseudotsuga menziesii)* and Sitka spruce *(Picea sitchensis)* are two of the dominant conifers of the Pacific Northwest where they form immense forests. The name Douglas fir, incidentally, is a

misnomer: this tree is not a true fir; its cones are pendant whereas the cones of true firs stand erect.

2. Coconut palm *(Cocos nucifera)*. Because their trunks are not woody but pulpy, palms are not considered trees in the botanical sense of the term. Several species are commercially valuable as suppliers of fruits and other substances—coconuts, copra, and dates; oils, liquids, sago, raffia, fiber, rattan, thatch, and even structural building materials. But the wild beauty of windswept fronds that curve and whisper in the slightest breeze sets palms apart from other trees.

3. Banana flower *(Musa sapientum)*. Banana "trees" are herbaceous plants which grow from tuber-like roots, reaching heights of fifteen to twenty feet. Their trunk-like stems are hollow cylinders formed by the concentrically overlapping bases of the huge leaves. Through this cylinder the root rhizome extends upward, terminating in the stalk which carries the flower and later the fruits. Each "tree" flowers only once during its life and bears only a single bunch of bananas, then dies. But its roots remain alive and, by sending up suckers, in time renew the plant.

4. Birches near Klockarberg in Dalarna, Sweden. Spring does not come to the forests of central Sweden until the end of May, but when it arrives, it is unique and spectacular. In the cool Nordic air, leaves unfurl so slowly that the woods do not get choked up with luscious greenery as in Connecticut. The forest remains open and airy, permitting long vistas of trees and the lovely cover of white anemones on the ground.

5. Beeches near Hälsingör, Denmark. Nowhere on earth, perhaps, is spring more welcome and its manifestations more moving than in the forests of the North. And the prize, I feel, should go to the Danish beech forests where the contrast between the smooth dark massive boles and branches and the sparse translucent green of the new leaves is indescribable.

6. Smokethorn, or smoketree *(Dalea spinosa)*. This native of the arid American Southwest is a typical desert plant, adapted to withstand extreme dryness and heat. To keep evaporation to a minimum, it is virtually leafless, and most of its branches are extremely thin, presenting very little surface to the sun.

7. Sycamore *(Platanus occidentalis)*. Photographed in early June, foliage is still sparse enough to reveal the characteristic framework of mighty limbs and curving branches which is part of its powerful "personality."

8-9. California live oak *(Quercus agrifolia)*. Barren hills covered with dry brown grass are a typical feature of the southern Californian landscape. This is the preferred habitat of the California live oak, a powerfully built tree with short thick trunk and widespread massive limbs, whose dome-shaped, dark green crowns rise from the gullies where moisture tends to collect, providing a welcome contrast to the yellow monotony of the heat-drenched sunburned hills.

10. White ash *(Fraxinus americana)*. Looming out of the winter fog, these "tree skeletons" are so typical that their pattern—the proportions between trunk and limbs, the stiff thrust of boughs, and the angle of branching—unmistakably spells "ash."

11. Young ash in the Adirondacks *(Fraxinus* sp.). To me, the whole wistful mood of autumn seems expressed in the claret hues and pastel shades of this tree as it stands in reddish splendor against the violet haze of the landscape. What a delightful contrast to see a tree that is not solid green!

12-13. Mojave yucca *(Yucca mohavensis)*. These tree-like "nontrees" are typical products of the desert. Dry and spiny, with tortured, twisting limbs and rustling dagger leaves, they surive on a minimum of water and a maximum of heat. These beautiful specimens are in the Sonoran Desert of Mexico.

14. Cabbage palm *(Sabal palmetto)*. A native of the southeastern United States, these palms grow like weeds along the muddy banks of Florida's Oklawaha River, forming jungles as dense and impenetrable as those of the Amazon.

15. Black birch *(Betula lenta)*, also called sweet birch because of the taste of its twigs and buds, or cherry birch because its bark is like that of cherry trees.

16. White ash *(Fraxinus americana)*. Their leaves already shed in preparation for winter, the trees stand like silent sentries in the gathering autumn dusk.

1▶

III
The Character of Trees

To recognize the characteristics that distinguish one species of tree from another is a matter of training. What at first seems a hopeless mess of green-on-green, or millions of leaves no two of which are alike, will gradually resolve itself into order. Here and there specific features will be learned and used for identification. Suddenly certain kinds of trees will look different from the rest: they will be recognized no matter where they are found; they will be named; they will become friends. Just as in human relationships one friendship leads to another, so identification of one species of trees leads to the recognition of others; the unknown gradually becomes familiar.

A few trees are so singular, so unlike all others in certain respects, that they can be recognized instantly in pictures even by people who have never seen one before. The following is an alphabetical list of twenty such trees, with the clue that leads to recognition and also the page number of the illustration of the respective tree, or typical part of it, noted in parentheses.

Banyan (adventitious roots that emerge from horizontal branches and grow into huge pillars; picture pages 108–109).

Beech (smooth gray bark that resembles cast aluminum; picture pages 72, 133–135).

Black locust (old trees have an unmistakably stark and gaunt silhouette and look as if they had been shelled in a war; massive, pole-like trunk and main limbs with disproportionately short branches; dark, deeply furrowed, diamond-patterned bark; delicate compound leaves with small elliptic leaflets of a grayish-green color different from that of most other leaves; sweet-smelling, white, pea-like flowers which produce leathery, three-inch pods; picture pages 31, 75).

Blue gum, the most commonly cultivated eucalyptus (bark peels off in long tattered strips; leaves are narrow and hard and give off aromatic fragrance when crushed; an evergreen broad-leaved tree imported from Australia now common in California and other frost-free regions; picture page 38).

Catalpa (conspicuous fruit pods look like large beans which stay on the tree through most of the winter; picture pages 24–25).

Ginkgo (fan-shaped leaves, often split deeply along one of the radiating veins; see the drawings in Chapter IX; photographs of the tree with its angular growth pattern on picture pages 30 and 37).

Horse-chestnut (five, sometimes seven, leaflets fan out like the spread fingers of a hand; clusters of white flowers arranged in a candelabra-like cone; golfball-sized, green, prickly fruit with large, shiny brown seeds; picture pages 22–23).

Live oak (old trees characterized by enormous massive limbs that reach out farther horizontally than those of any other tree; small, leathery, glossy, dark green leaves; an evergreen typical of the American South; picture pages 52–56).

Mulberry (several differently shaped leaves—unlobed, mitten-shaped, three-lobed, and multi-lobed—growing on the same tree; leaf edges have coarse round teeth; see the drawings in Chapter IX and the photograph on picture page 82).

Paper birch (pure white, chalky bark that peels off easily in paper-thin strips; picture pages 4, 67).

Pin oak (the only oak whose lower branches always are angled downward; picture page 27).

Royal palm (the trunk looks as though it is made of poured concrete; picture pages 40, 51).

Sassafras (three differently shaped leaves—unlobed, mitten-shaped, and three-lobed—growing on the same tree; leaf edges are smooth; see drawings in Chapter IX and photograph on picture page 86).

Sausage tree (unique fruits look like large, dangling sausages; pictures page 51).

Shagbark hickory (bark of old trees comes off in the form of long, hard, curving strips that resemble warped shingles nailed to the side of a house; picture pages 21, 69).

Strangler fig (grows out of the side of a host tree which it eventually "strangles" to death; picture pages 110–111).

Sweet gum (star-shaped leaves; bristly spherical fruit hangs into winter; picture page 83).

Sycamore (bark peels off in patches of green, yellow, and brown, giving the impression of a geological relief map; fruit dangling from thread-like stalks looks like little spheres on a Christmas tree: if only one ball per stalk, the tree is an American sycamore; if two or more, it is a London Plane tree; picture pages 7, 45, 50, 149).

Tulip tree (uniquely shaped leaf has notched or "inverted" tip; see the drawings in Chapter IX and the photographs on picture pages 46, 88, 89).

Weeping willow (long, slender branches hang straight down like long hair, often touching the ground; picture pages 28–29).

The twenty trees listed above have such unmistakable "personalities" that anyone can recognize them at first glance. In this respect they are unique. Most trees require a second, closer look for proper identification. Many, however, can easily be identified as belonging to a specific group; for example, the red

apply. Making the right choice is usually simple and will, via a reference number, lead the student to the next choice. And so it goes until the final choice, when the dauntless pursuer is rewarded with the name of the tree.

This "yes" or "no" choice which, in essence, is the same as the binary principle according to which electronic computers operate, is based on the fact that all the trees in the world can be classified as belonging to a few large groups which in turn can be split into smaller groups which again can be broken down into still smaller groups, and so on. The principles which underlie such systems of classification vary. They may be scientific, in which case the breakdown would progress from a few large *orders*, to *families*, to *genera*, and

oaks with their typical pinnately lobed, bristle-tipped leaves (see drawing above) which are often so similar that even an expert might not be able to identify the tree as belonging to a specific species merely on the basis of a leaf. In this particular case the fruit, flowers, or twigs must be examined before a more exact identification can be made.

The ability to recognize a specific tree as belonging to a particular group is, in essence, a process of elimination—*knowing what it cannot be*. Most popular tree-identification books are organized in accordance with this principle. From the first to the last, the reader is offered two or more choices, only one of which can

finally *species*. However, although this is the only scientifically acceptable system of classification, its successful use presupposes specialized knowledge which the layman usually does not possess. Consequently, popular identification books are generally organized on the basis of "clues" that require no special knowledge. One very good and inexpensive guide, for example, is based solely on the shapes of leaves (the *Tree Finder*, published by Nature Study Guild, Naperville, Illinois). Another uses twigs, winter buds, and leaf scars as means of recognition and is therefore particularly useful in identifying deciduous trees in winter or early spring when leaves are unavailable.

Other books use still other clues, or combinations of clues.

Students without any training in botany should start with the simplest kinds of clues, such as the way in which a tree grows. In this respect, three different growth patterns can be distinguished:

Spire-like trees (*excurrent* growth pattern) have a single pole-like trunk with relatively thin lateral branches; branches at the same height from the ground are usually arranged in a whorl. This is the growth pattern typical of most *conifers*—the "softwoods" or "evergreens" with needle-like leaves, such as spruce, fir, pine, etc.—but is found occasionally among certain broad-leaved trees such as ash, maple, and ginkgo, particularly when they are young.

but exactly what is it? How can we find the sub-group to which it belongs? We examine its leaves—its "needles"—which may belong to one of four sub-groups: needle-like, scale-like, awl-like with sharp tips, or a combination of awl-like and scale-like "leaves" occurring on the same tree. In the first case the tree belongs to one of the following sub-groups: the pines, larches, spruces, firs, or cypresses. In the second it may be a cedar, a cypress, or a juniper. In the third it is a juniper, and in the fourth red cedar. Let us say our tree has needle-like leaves. We look at its needles more closely. Do they grow in bundles or groups, or are they attached singly to the twig? In the first case, our tree may belong to the pines or the larches; in the second case, it must be a spruce, fir, hemlock, cypress, or yew. Assuming our tree fits this second case, we

Spreading trees (*deliquescent* growth pattern) have trunks that are repeatedly divided and subdivided, with trunk and crown merging imperceptibly. Branches may be almost as large and massive as the trunk. This is the growth pattern typical of most broad-leaved trees such as maple, apple, or oak, although, when young, a few broad-leaved trees grow in a spire-like pattern.

Columnar trees (*columnar* growth pattern) have a branchless trunk which carries a crown of leaves at its top. This growth pattern is found exclusively in palms.

Now let us assume that a tree which we want to identify belongs to the first group: it is an evergreen with a single pole-like trunk and relatively thin lateral branches arranged in whorls. It obviously is a conifer,

look again at its needles. Are they more or less four-sided in cross section so that they can be rolled easily between forefinger and thumb? If so, our tree is a spruce. Or, are the needles flat so that they cannot be rolled between two fingers? If so, our tree is either a fir, hemlock, cypress, or yew. Assuming that the needles are flat, to which one of these four genera does our tree belong? The simplest way to find out is to examine its cones: if they stand erect, pointing toward the sky, the tree is a fir; if they are quite small, soft, dangling, and in great profusion, the tree is a hemlock; if the cones are relatively small, hard, and more or less spherical, the tree is a cypress; and if it has no cones at all, but carries instead berry-like fruits, it is a yew.

In this way, through elimination of *what a tree cannot be* on the basis of "clues" given in any tree-identification book, one will eventually arrive at the name of a given tree.

A note of warning: the foregoing attempt at showing how to identify a tree is of necessity a simplified presentation which applies in principle, but not necessarily in every detail. There are frequent exceptions to what at first may appear to be ironclad rules. For instance, the growth pattern of conifers, particularly cypresses and junipers, is not always spire-like and not all evergreens have needles or scales, since some, such as the live oaks, magnolias, figs, although "evergreens," are broad-leaved trees. Such exceptions are of course mentioned at the proper places in any tree-identification book. Here I only intend to show how tree recognition proceeds from the general to the particular; how order is brought into chaos.

Since leaves are important to tree identification, it might be assumed that deciduous trees—those that shed their leaves in the fall—can be identified only when they are in foliage. This, of course, is not true. As already mentioned, broad-leaved trees, if necessary, can be identified solely on the basis of twigs, winter buds, and leaf scars—clues that are available even when the trees are bare. As a matter of fact, winter is a particularly good time for studying deciduous trees because growth pattern stands out. (Incidentally, if a deciduous tree, and particularly a young one, retains its dead leaves through most of the winter and sometimes into spring, it is either an oak or a beech. Dead oak leaves are brown, leathery, and lobed; oak bark is ridged and rough. Dead beech leaves are a pale, pinkish sand color, oval and toothed; beech bark is silver-gray and smooth.) Although no two trees of the same species are ever alike to the same extent as, say, two squirrels or two bluejays, they nevertheless possess a subtle likeness that can perhaps best be described by saying that their "character" or "personality" is unmistakably the same. To the sensitive or trained eye a white oak, for example, unmistakably "looks" like a white oak, even from afar or in winter when it has no leaves, and *not* like a beech, an ash, or any other kind of tree. These subtle characteristics which give a tree its "personality" are particularly clear when the trees are bare. It is for this reason that studying "tree skeletons" cannot be recommended strongly enough to anyone with more than a cursory interest in trees.

The silhouettes on the opposite page illustrate typical growth patterns of some of our most common trees. They were traced over actual photographs and show, in slightly simplified form, ever so much more clearly than pictures of the same trees in foliage, what is typical of each. Better than long descriptions, such silhouettes reveal the subtle differences between kinds of trees manifested, for example, in the proportion between height and spread; thickness of branches in relation to the trunk; straightness or curving of limbs; angles at which branches leave the trunk; and other "clues" which unmistakably tell you that this can only be an oak, this is a hickory, this must be an elm.

But now I must again sound a note of caution: only trees growing in open surroundings have clear-cut "personalities." Forest-grown trees, or trees whose style has been cramped by other nearby trees, cannot express their personalities as clearly as these solitary beauties and are, as a rule, taller, skinnier, less spreading and less luxurious. By this I do not mean that they have no "character," because they most certainly do; but their character is more subdued, less easily recognized. To identify such trees positively it is usually necessary to look for confirming evidence: leaves, bark, flowers, fruits. For example, even in winter leaves can give a clue to the identity of deciduous trees: the dead leaves lying on the ground. If a winter-bare tree has all the characteristics of, say, an oak, and we find the typical leaves of chestnut oak at its base, we have at least circumstantial evidence that our tree is a chestnut oak. Or, if exceptionally large, shiny, sticky, winter buds top each twig of a tree whose branches grow in a characteristically curving and waving pattern (see picture page 22), we can be sure it is a horse-chestnut. Or, if the bark of what seems to be a birch flakes off in thin, tough, chalky-white strips, we know that it is a paperbirch (see the picture on page 67) and not a gray birch or a yellow birch. Or if the pith of the twigs is chambered (see Chapter VII), we have found either a black walnut, a butternut, a black gum, or a paulownia. Clues such as these are listed in any good tree identification book. But it is fun to anticipate the clues, and it fills one with a sense of pride to be able to spot a tree correctly from a distance merely on the basis of something as intangible as "character" or, to use the proper scientific term, physiognomy.

Growth patterns of trees. Top: Elm, white oak, shagbark hickory. Bottom: ginkgo, sugar maple, pin oak.

Picture pages 17–31

17. English oak (*Quercus robur*). Although this majestic tree stands in Dyrehaven Park outside Copenhagen, it seems to personify the essence of the "German Oak"—a symbol of strength and endurance. The "personality" of this tree is unmistakably oak—no other European tree grows so old, its trunk and boughs so massive, its branches so gnarled, or its bark so deeply ridged. And even though some of its major limbs are gone and others dead, it still stands as strong as ever, a rock among lesser trees, a symbol of tenacity and power.

18–19. Sugar maple (*Acer saccharum*). The same tree,

photographed once in summer, again in winter. Seeing these two views side by side is like seeing an ordinary and an X-ray photograph. And of the two, the latter is the more revealing: many trees have dome-shaped crowns, but the branching pattern of a typical sugar maple such as this expresses its character—it is different from that of any other tree. You will realize this instantly if you compare this picture with the previous one and the two that follow. Familiarize yourself with these four growth patterns—specifically, the angles at which branches emerge from the trunk and the proportions between trunk and branches—and you will never again confuse these trees with one another, but instead will recognize each, even at a distance.

20. American elm *(Ulmus americana)*. The nearly parallel upward thrust and subsequent graceful outward curving of the major limbs, which arch and subdivide and spray back to earth like an umbrella of water rising from a fountain, are characteristic of this tree.

21. Shagbark hickory *(Carya ovata)*. Disproportionately thin branches angling off and stretching more or less horizontally from the usually undivided trunk typify the growth pattern of this tree. Mature specimens can be recognized further by their bark (see picture page 69), which is characterized by long, hard, gray strips that have become partly detached, curving outward like warped wooden shingles. The large compound leaves have five or seven leaflets, of which the one at the tip is the largest.

22. Horse-chestnut *(Aesculus hippocastanum)* in Nymphenburger Park near Munich, Germany.

23. Flowering horse-chestnut trees in Ribe, Denmark. Growth pattern is characterized by wildly curving branches that wave up and down like a roller coaster. Leaves that bring to mind a hand with five or seven fingers, candelabra-like white flowers dotted with red and yellow spots, and, later in the year, round, prickly green fruits containing the leathery "chestnut," make this tree easy to identify.

24–25. Catalpa *(Catalpa bignonioides)*. Three characteristics combine to give this tree its unmistakable character: unusually large, thin, smooth-edged, heart-shaped leaves arranged in pairs or whorls of three; big clusters of white, trumpet-like flowers with ruffled and scalloped petals dotted with brown and purple spots; and, in fall, masses of bean-like, dangling fruit pods that sometimes remain on the tree throughout the winter.

26. Red maple *(Acer rubrum)*. The name is aptly chosen; at all times of the year this tree displays something red. In winter the twigs are reddish, the buds crimson; in spring masses of tiny flowers weave a reddish halo around its crown; in summer red leaf stalks justify its name; and in fall the foliage of no other tree turns a brighter red than that of a red maple (see also picture page 144). The specimen shown in this photograph is unusually large—normally red maples do not grow quite so big. This tree stands near Roxbury, Connecticut.

27. Pin oak *(Quercus palustris)*. A tree very easy to identify: its lower branches grow downward!

28–29. Weeping willow *(Salix babylonica)*. This Old World import is instantly recognized by its extremely long, slender twigs and branchlets that hang straight down, forming shimmering cascades of leaves that sometimes touch the ground. Usually found near water and never on dry soil.

30. Ginkgo *(Ginkgo biloba)*. The growth pattern of this tree, a native of China, always reminds me of a pagoda: its main branches, which stiffly angle off the trunk at approximately forty-five degrees, seem to imitate the upthrust of curving eaves. The trunk is strangely conical instead of primarily cylindrical like the trunks of most other trees. Because of their resistance to polluted air, ginkgos are widely planted as street trees. As a result, this rarest and most unique of all trees, which is no longer found wild anywhere, is more familiar to many people than some of our most common native trees, which have less tolerance for dirty city air.

31. Black locust *(Robinia pseudo-acacia)*. The stark, almost grim silhouette of this species is unmistakable: pole-like trunks rise straight and uncompromising as columns clad in deeply furrowed bark; main branches are massive and sharply angular, secondary branches disproportionately thin.

26

IV
The Oldest Living Things

Some bristlecone pines are the oldest living things on earth. Virtually immortal, these unique trees look strikingly different because most of the older specimens are only partly alive—lush and living dark green branches combine with yellow, brown, and black deadwood. At first sight they convey the impression of immense age.

An article by the late Dr. Edmund Schulman in the March 1958 issue of the *National Geographic Magazine* first aroused my interest in bristlecone pines. Dr. Schulman, a dendrochronologist and climatologist who at that time was associated with the Laboratory of Tree-Ring Research of the University of Arizona in Tucson, gave a stirring account of the drama and excitement that surrounded his discovery of the first living organisms whose age could be proved by scientific methods to exceed 4,000 years. This was no longer guesswork—subjective impressions based only on spectacular dimensions—but hard fact supported by indisputable evidence: the number of annual growth rings counted in the examined trees. Since then a total of seventeen bristlecone pines have been found which, living and still growing, are over 4,000 years old, the oldest some 4,600 years old.

Imagine a tree so old that it began life 2,635 years before the birth of Christ. It germinated when the great Assyrian kings ruled Babylon and Nineveh, but it seems certain that no human being had yet penetrated the harsh and silent world where, in the heart of the High Sierra at an altitude of 11,300 feet, the tiny seedling sprouted which, several millennia later, was to be proclaimed the oldest living thing on earth.

The Mesopotamian city-states vanished beneath the shifting sands of the rivers that had made them rich and great, and Egypt emerged as the most powerful nation of the civilized world. But by the time the great pyramids were being built, our tiny seedling

had already grown into a mighty tree some 1,400 years old. Another 1,300 years went by—the birth of Christ. Empires rose and fell, but our bristlecone pine kept on growing, steadily increasing in size by adding to its trunk and branches year after year a microscopically thin layer of wood. When the Crusaders set out to liberate the Holy City Jerusalem, our tree was already 3,740 years old. Some 860 years later, when the first man orbited the earth, it was still clinging to life although now a mere ruin of a tree, a gnarled jagged piece of deadwood the color and texture of sculptured bronze, overlaid on one side by a narrow strip of living bark barely sufficient to connect the few remaining living roots with its few remaining living branches. But the sap still rises every year when the snow melts and the sun stands high in the sky, and a paper-thin layer of new wood is added to the living side of the trunk. And there it stands, firmly implanted in the rock-strewn ground, growing where nothing else can grow, fighting the winter storms and surviving the almost unimaginable cold, the hardiest, toughest, oldest living thing on earth.

The only place in the world where bristlecone pines grow is the American Southwest, and the best place to see them is the Ancient Bristlecone Pine Forest in the White Mountain District of the Inyo National Forest in California. A visit to this unusual forest was to be the highlight of the trip which I made in 1966 to complete the photographs for this book. My expectations were surpassed, even though I had only a short time before spent a couple of weeks in the redwood and sequoia forests and been overwhelmed by these unbelievably immense trees. But although bristlecone pines are quite small—the largest specimens hardly exceed forty feet in height—their fantastic forms and spectacular habitat combine to leave still stronger impressions.

The trip started south from Bishop, California, toward the town of Big Pine, along highway 395. Half a mile north of Big Pine we turned off on Westgard Pass Road. Westgard Pass Road follows an old mining trail past the ruins of a wooden tollhouse at Batchelder Spring, the only water source along the entire road, and for fourteen miles twists and climbs among the foothills to Cedar Flat. Here the road forks, the right-hand branch leading over Westgard Pass to Goldfield, the lefthand branch going to the bristlecone pines. The new road is narrower, bumpier, and considerably steeper, but nothing compared to what lay ahead. From time to time, openings in the nearby hills permitted spectacular views across the length and breadth of Owens Valley which lay about a mile below us, with the snow peaks of the Sierra rising 10,000 feet above the valley floor. Seven miles of this road brought us to the Ancient Bristlecone Pine Forest and Schulman Grove.

At Schulman Grove we found a nearly pure stand of bristlecone pines, a tourist information booth (which was closed since it was still too early in the season), and, half a mile's walk from the road, Pine Alpha, the first bristlecone pine discovered whose age had been established by ring count as exceeding 4,000 years (this still living tree was found to be 4,300 years old). Age, incidentally, is established by drilling through the bark into the heart of the tree with a hollow, tube-like tool called an "increment borer," extracting the thin, dowelstick-like core of wood, and counting the annual growth rings. This procedure does not hurt the tree since the narrow drill hole soon fills with resin and seals itself. But impressive as Pine Alpha was—a shattered, blasted hulk of yellow and black deadwood some four feet wide and eighteen feet high with a ten-inch strip of living bark running up one side to sustain its few green branches—I did not like the background for photographs and decided to go all the way to the end of the trail, to the Patriarch Grove, although I had been warned by the District Ranger that the going would be rough.

He was right. Very soon the road began to deteriorate into what can only be called a jeep track, and for the next twelve miles we never got out of first gear. Wysse, who has more patience than I, drove all the way, and she did a marvelous job of conserving the strength and tires of our ten-year old Ford on a road that, for the most part, was nothing short of murderous for both car and driver. Stretches of slithery ankle-deep dust alternated with miles of track densely covered with shattered rocks that threatened to shred our tires and boulders that had to be avoided lest we crack the crankcase or bend a

wheel. Higher and higher we drove on a trail that was like a roller coaster, over grades so steep that, every time we reached a peak and craned our necks to peer across the hood of our car into the next valley, we hesitated to go on for fear that our car might not be able to climb out of that infernal hole over inclines that seemed to go straight up into the sky. For traction on the rubble-covered track is negligible and wheelspin means death to the tires, not to mention the fact that at an altitude of some 11,000 feet the power of the engine is considerably lessened. The thought of a breakdown in this unbelievably lonely moon landscape miles away from civilization was not a pleasant one. But we got through, and after an hour and a half of driving at an average speed of eight miles an hour arrived on a high plateau. There, on the slope across the valley in a landscape of breathtaking grandeur, stood the trees we had crossed a continent to see.

Thinking back to that moment and looking at my photographs I realize that this experience cannot be conveyed by means of pictures and words. Too many intangibles contributed to it: the nightmare drive filled with a sense of expectancy and tingling adventure; the change in temperature from a stifling 90 degrees plus in the valley to a cool 35 degrees at 11,300 feet which, due to the burning sun, felt pleasant; the thin air which made our heads spin, and, above all, that indescribably exhilarating feeling of standing at the top of the world.

All around us, ringing the horizon, glittered and sparkled the snowcapped peaks of the High Sierra, rising blindingly white 14,000 feet into the azure of the early summer sky. The thin cold air felt heavenly after the humid heat of the valley, and the starkness of the landscape at timberline, where the ground was bare except for shattered rock, made us feel like the last remaining human beings on earth. Never before had I experienced such an overwhelming feeling of remoteness, such a sense of detachment, such an awareness of the presence of something unimaginably big and eternal, as at this moment, standing on one of the highest plateaus on the North American continent face to face with the oldest living things on earth.

We took our photographic gear and slowly walked across the dip and up the slope toward the scattered old trees, where we spent the two most memorable hours of our entire trip.

Bristlecone pines are small as trees go. They usually are short and squat, and their height seldom exceeds thirty-five feet. But like no other tree, they give impressions of immense tenacity and strength. Young bristlecone pines are often beautifully symmetrical (see picture page 32), their needles a rich, deep green. And when you step up to one and gently stroke it you find that it is not harsh and prickly as you might expect, but soft as a furry animal's bushy tail, a fact which explains one of this remarkable tree's popular names—Foxtail Pine. Because of the severe climatic conditions under which the trees live—they are found mainly at elevations from 7,000 to 11,000 feet—bristlecone pines are, of course, slow-growing. How slow can be realized by Dr. Schulman's discovery of a tree that was only three feet high, had a trunk three inches thick, yet was some 700 years old according to a count of its annual growth rings. Understandably, these growth rings are extremely fine—often there are more than a hundred per inch—and must, of course, be counted under a microscope. How these rings can be made to yield an accurate year by year account of the climatic conditions over the past 6,000 years is a fantastic story that will be told in Chapter XIII.

The most spectacular trees are, of course, those whose wood is partly exposed. They stand on the stony slopes like monuments cast in bronze. The color of their trunks and limbs is a metallic yellow, orange, brown and black mixed and blended as if molten brass, copper and iron had been drawn together while still in a plastic state. Their forms, which have none of the softness of wood, call to mind the spiky sharpness of metal. Their fine-grained texture—the result of the wood's extreme hardness and its centuries of exposure to ice and storm and blasting sand—produces, when you run your fingertips over these dead limbs, sensations of polished metal.

Thin veils of haze began to condense high in the sky while I exposed my last roll of color film. The sun disappeared, and it suddenly became cold. A harsh wind started blowing from the ice fields, and snow flurries began to fill the air. The silent sentries, which for millennia had stared sightlessly toward the snowy heights of the Sierra, gradually faded behind a slowly thickening curtain of snow as we walked back to our car, turned it around, and carefully nosed our way back to civilization.

Picture pages 32–36

Bristlecone pines *(Pinus aristata)*. Photographed in the Ancient Bristlecone Pine Forest, White Mountain District, Inyo National Forest, California, at an elevation of 11,300 feet.

V
The Structure of Trees

Some three hundred years ago, in an attempt to find out what trees are made of and whether Aristotle's idea that they derive their food from the earth was true, the Flemish physician and chemist J. B. van Helmont (1577–1644) performed an experiment. He planted a young willow in a tub filled with earth and accurately weighed both the tree and the soil. For five years he added nothing but water to the tub. Then he carefully removed the willow, complete with all its roots, from the tub and weighed both the tree and the soil. To his surprise, he found that the weight of the soil had decreased by only two ounces, although the tree, not counting five years' shedded leaves, had added more than 164 pounds to its original weight. Van Helmont rightly concluded that only a minute amount of the substance of the tree had come from the soil, while the major part must have been supplied by water and air.

Wood certainly does not look as though it is made of water and air—it is neither liquid nor gaseous but heavy, substantial stuff. Nevertheless, that these are the components of wood can be proved easily by burning wood in a fireplace: at the end of several days of burning and the consumption of perhaps a hundred pounds of wood, all that is left are a few handfuls of fluffy, almost weightless ashes—the mineral components of the tree; the "substantial stuff" has burned. Since well-seasoned logs are relatively dry, already having lost most of their water content through evaporation, what is left—the dry wood—must have come from the air. It is indeed carbon, which the tree has taken from the atmosphere in the form of carbon dioxide and used to build its tissues. During the burning process this carbon combines once more with oxygen to form carbon dioxide and escapes into the air as a gas, returning to the great reservoir from which it came.

No matter whether we examine its root, trunk, branches, flowers, seeds, or leaves, we will of course find that a tree, like all other living organisms, consists of cells. Although fundamentally all cells are alike, plant cells vary enormously in size. The smallest plant cells—certain kinds of spherical bacteria, each bacterium consisting of a single cell that is a complete plant—are only .00002 inches in diameter. The largest, those of the bark of a ramie, a tropical plant, can be over twenty inches long. Because they are usually in tight contact with one another, most plant cells are flattened on all sides by the pressure of their neighbors and are therefore many-sided. Others are irregular, spherical, cylindrical, or brick- or spindle-shaped.

Despite their normally "microscopic" size, cells are very complex, and in many respects mysterious, structures. Imagine a chemical factory—one fully equipped to manufacture a large number of highly complex products ranging from building materials and processed foods to pigments and vitamins, complete with storage spaces for raw materials and finished products, with power generators and an automatic command center—reduced to the size of the dot of this "i." The structure envisioned would still be simple in comparison to that of a cell, not to mention that, unlike the cell, it could neither grow nor reproduce itself. No wonder that an understanding of the nature of life has so far eluded our most intense efforts.

Fundamentally, all plant cells consist of *protoplasm* enclosed within a thin membrane, the whole usually surrounded by a cell wall. Protoplasm is the very essence of life. It is a viscous, semitransparent substance, 75 to 90 per cent water. The remaining percentage is mostly protein mixed with some fatty compounds and other organic and inorganic components, salts, and gases. Chemically, protoplasm is a *colloid*—a suspension of minute particles in a supporting medium structurally (but not chemically) similar to milk, gelatin, or glue.

The most important part of protoplasm—as of every living cell—is the *nucleus*. The nucleus is the center which controls all the cell's metabolic activities. At the same time, it is the carrier of the *chromosomes*, which harbor the *genes*, the controllers of heredity. Remove its nucleus, and the cell invariably dies.

The nucleus is suspended in a viscous substance called *cytoplasm*, the undifferentiated, nonspecialized portion of the protoplasm. In addition to the nucleus, the cytoplasm contains a number of other specialized structures with a diversity of functions: to manufacture or store food for the plant; to produce energy; to provide colorants for flowers and fruit; to make vitamins; or to perform other functions necessary to the welfare of the tree. And finally, there are one or several bubble-like spaces called *vacuoles* within the cytoplasm which are filled with nonliving cell sap, a complex solution of a great variety of substances including the red, blue, and purple pigments that color flowers, fruit, and autumn leaves.

Cells perpetuate themselves by a division process called *mitosis*. We can witness this process under the microscope, although nobody has so far been able to discover what causes it, or even why it should occur at all. The first signs of imminent cell division are structural changes within its nucleus. Molecules consisting of nucleic acids previously distributed at random begin to condense as if under the influence of a magnetic field, arranging themselves in slender, coiled threads, the *chromosomes*. These threads are the chains of genes which in the precise and normally unvarying arrangement of their molecules carry in coded form the entire plan for the future animal or plant down to the last minute detail such as the color of the eyes of a man, the dots and lines and curlicues on the wings of a moth, the downy fuzz that covers the underside of a leaf, or the heady fragrance of a flower. Imagine what this implies: thousands of different qualities precisely specified and ready for future execution condensed within a speck of matter too small to be seen except under the most powerful microscope!

Each chromosome splits lengthwise into two identical halves, duplicating itself molecule for molecule, doubling the number of threads. Then, as the rest of the nucleus dissolves within the cytoplasm, the previously coiled chromosomes straighten out and align themselves in two identical sets of fibers. Slowly, these fibers contract, and the two groups pull apart, each forming the center of a new nucleus. A new wall appears between the two nuclei, and, where previously there was only one cell, there are now two. Again each cell carries within its chromosomes a complete set of instructions which will in time enable it to duplicate itself, always remaining the same kind of living organism, passing on its living plasm to the next generation, be it a maple, a mouse, or a man.

Thus, in a sense the germ cells of all living things at least are immortal, and every single-celled organism may be said to be at least 2,000 million years old. We still carry enshrined within the structures of heredity the spark of life that first ignited billions of years ago. Once kindled, it never died, and, by dividing again and again, it multiplied, passing on the essence of life from one generation to the next, forming link after link of a chain that will not end as long as the sun describes its path in the sky.

Although fundamentally alike, cells differ greatly in details of construction, each type being adapted to the function it has to perform. The cells of a leaf, for example, are quite unlike those of wood or bark, and these again differ from the cells of a root or flower. Normally, aggregations of similar cells form groups, groups combine to form tissue, and tissues of different kinds make up the organs of a plant.

The organs of a tree

A tree is sometimes compared to a machine—a light-machine driven by solar energy. Actually, this comparison is inadequate because a tree also has aspects of an entire factory and even a city. Any tree contains a number of enormously complex yet marvelously functional systems designed to serve a variety of purposes, each vital to its welfare: to anchor the tree to the ground; to take water from the earth or carbon from the air; to pump water to the highest leaf; to produce food for the entire tree; to move this food from the place where it is produced throughout the rest of the plant; to dispose of waste products; to reproduce the tree; and so forth. A tree has developed special organs to fulfill these diverse functions. Here is a listing in capsule form:

The root. Every tree has an underground root system whose main purpose is twofold: to anchor the tree securely to the ground, and to take water and minerals in solution from the earth. More information on the roots of trees is given in Chapter XI.

The trunk of a tree has three main functions: to raise the crown of the tree high above the lesser plants in order to expose the leaves more fully to the sun; to provide the rigid columnar structure for the attachment of limbs and branches; and to accommodate the system of pipelines required for the vertical and lateral transport of water and sap. (See Chapters VII and XIII.)

The limbs, branches, and twigs, which together form the *crown* of the tree, are woody structures that support the leaves, flowers, and fruit. They also contain the *vascular bundles* which conduct water and nutrients from the roots to the leaves and flowers and distribute food manufactured by the leaves to other parts of the tree.

The leaves, by the process of *photosynthesis,* manufacture the food which sustains the tree and enables it to grow. Photosynthesis, a process mastered only by green plants, is the vital basis on which all animal life on earth depends; without green plants neither animals nor man could exist. Every molecule of every bit of animal tissue is built around atoms of carbon. But although carbon is a constituent of the atmosphere, animals, unlike plants, cannot absorb it from the air by breathing, but can obtain it only by eating plants. Plant-eating animals get their vital carbon directly from the plants they consume; flesh-eating animals obtain their carbon by eating animals that have fed on plants. More information on the structure and functions of leaves is in Chapter IX.

The flowers are the reproductive organs of a tree. They produce the seeds from which new trees eventually arise. Seed formation is based on fertilization, i.e., the union of *gametes* (male and female sex cells) to produce a *zygote,* the fertilized egg. The zygote is the first cell of the future tree. It grows into an embryo within the seed and will, after germination, give rise to the adult tree. Although the flowers of many trees are inconspicuous, small, and drab, those of others are large and beautiful. Most people know and enjoy the flowers of horsechestnut and catalpa, of magnolia and tulip trees, and especially those of fruit trees. Apple-blossom time is a sure harbinger of spring, and Washington's flowering Japanese cherry trees are a world-famous annual attraction.

A flower consists of a number of different parts only two of which are directly involved in seed production: the *stamen* and the *pistil.* Stamens are the male sex organs of a plant; they produce the *pollen grains* which

give rise to male gametes. Pistils are the female sex organs of a plant; in their enlarged lower part, the *ovary,* they harbor the *ovules,* each of which contains an *egg.* During pollination pollen grains are deposited, usually either by pollinating insects or by the wind, on the pistil where they germinate and form pollen tubes which rapidly grow downward through the entire length of the pistil until they reach the ovary. Through these pollen tubes the male gametes descend to fuse with the egg.

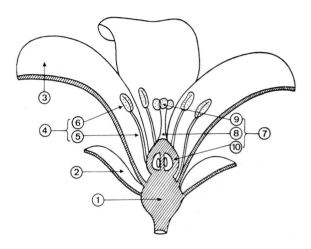

Schematical cross-section of a perfect flower. 1—Receptacle; 2—sepal; 3—petal; 4—stamen; 5—filament; 6—anther; 7—pistil; 8—style; 9—stigma; 10—ovary with ovules.

A perfect flower (such as an apple blossom) consists of the following parts: the base by which it is attached to the stalk is the *receptacle.* Out of the receptacle grow a number of floral organs which are always arranged in the same order. The outermost of these are the *sepals,* usually small green leaf-like structures which collectively make up the *calyx.* Next in order come the *petals,* normally the most conspicuous and colorful parts of a flower which, taken together, are the *corolla.* Calyx and corolla together are called the *perianth.* Within the circle of the petals, arranged in an inner ring, are the *stamens* (the male organs) each of which consists of two parts: a thin, elongated stalk called the *filament* carries at its top the sac-like *anther,* the producer of the pollen grains. Finally, from the very heart of the flower rises the *pistil* (the female organ), usually a flask-shaped structure consisting of three main parts: the stalk-like *style* which terminates in the receiver of the pollen grains, the *stigma* (often sticky, rough, or feathery), and a hollow expanded base, the *ovary*, which contains the *ovules* which after fertilization develop into *seeds*.

We must distinguish among three types of flowers in regard to sex. If both stamens and pistils are present within the same flower, it is termed *bisexual* or *perfect*. If *either* the stamens, *or* the pistil, are absent, the flower is *unisexual* or *imperfect*. Flowers that have *only stamens* (but lack a pistil) are male and are called *staminate*. Conversely, flowers that *possess a pistil* (but lack stamens) are female and are called *pistillate*.

Similarly, we must distinguish among three different types of tree: trees which bear *perfect flowers* (such as the apple) are termed *polygamous*. Trees in which staminate and pistillate flowers occur *together* (oaks, beeches, birches, hickory, and walnut trees) are termed *monoecious*. And trees which are *either* male *or* female, i.e., in which staminate and pistillate flowers *occur on different* plants of the same species but *not together* (ailanthus, ashes, ginkgo, holly, poplars, willows), are called *dioecious*.

Although the flowers of all *Angiosperms* are constructed according to the same plan, modifications are common and details may vary widely. Take, for example, the dogwood: the lovely white "petals" of its showy flowers are not petals at all but *bracts*, modified leaves (they are much coarser than petals) which encircle a cluster of small, inconspicuous flowers which nobody would notice in the absence of these bracts. Or look at maple trees in spring: the green-yellow or reddish sheen which surrounds these trees like a halo is not caused, as most people assume, by budding leaves, but by the flowers of these trees which, though small and inconspicuous, are built according to the typical pattern of all *Angiosperms*.

In contrast, the flowers of *Gymnosperms* are different, simpler, more primitive. The conifers, our "softwoods," for example, reproduce themselves by means of cone-like organs, the *strobili* (singular: *strobilus*), aggregations of *sporophylls* which are modified, spore-producing leaves, remnants of their ancient lineage. Two kinds of strobili exist, *pollen cones* and *seed cones*. The pollen cones are small, usually inconspicuous but

sometimes bright red or yellow organs which last only a few days in order to shed their pollen to be borne by the wind to the seed cones. After fertilization, the seed cones develop into the well-known woody structures popularly called "pine cones" which produce the seeds. The size of the seed cones varies greatly, and it is interesting to note that the tallest of all trees, the redwood, produces some of the smallest cones with an average length of slightly less than an inch. Typical sequoia cones measure somewhere between two and three inches. The largest cones are those of the sugar pine, which can reach a length of more than twenty inches.

Flowers are one of the most valuable aids in plant classification. Their construction often provides the botanist with clues to their evolutionary origin, guiding him to group related species and classify them according to their origin in an ascending line that starts with the most primitive and ends with the most advanced and specialized forms. For example: the yuccas on picture pages 12–13 belong to the lily family, the locust on picture page 31 is a relative of the pea, and apple trees are related to roses.

The fruits of trees vary enormously in regard to structure, form, size, material, and color. Botanically speaking a fruit is any ripened plant ovary (or group of ovaries) together with any closely associated flower part that may be fused with the ovary at maturity. Here is a listing of different types of tree fruit:

Simple fruits consist entirely of the ripened ovary with no other part of the flower included. This type of fruit may be either dry or fleshy. Simple dry fruits are, among others: *The legume*, a pod that often opens along two opposite sides and is familiar to everyone as peapods and beanpods; this is the fruit of the black locust and honey locust, both of which belong to the pea family, and of redbud, Kentucky coffeetree, etc. *The capsule*, a pod-like fruit which may open in a variety of ways; known to all is the three-valved capsule of the horse-chestnut; the valves open at maturity to release a single large seed, the delight of children, the shiny "chestnut." *The nut*, a type of fruit that, unlike those previously listed, does not open when ripe; the term "nut" is applied to any fruit which at maturity is hard, woody, or stony; however, not all nuts are simple fruits. (Brazil nuts, for example, are not true nuts, but large seeds originally [i.e., before marketing] enclosed in a large, spherical shell five to six inches in diameter, each shell harboring anywhere from twelve to twenty-four individual seeds, each seed covered by a hard, woody, shell-like seed coat.)

Simple fleshy fruits are, among others: *The berry*, a fruit in which, after ripening, the entire ovary wall—the *pericarp*—is still fleshy and often edible; typical tree fruits belonging to this type are the date, avocado, and citrus fruits although, in the latter, the pericarp—the peel or rind—is usually not eaten except in the form of marmalade. *The drupe*, a fleshy fruit in which the pericarp is separated into a fleshy outer portion and a hard inner part—the pit or stone—which in turn contains the seed; typical representatives are the peach, plum, cherry, almond, and olive. *Accessory fruits*, which are produced if other parts of the flower have fused with the ripened ovary wall and thus become an integral part of the fruit. *The pome*, a special type of accessory fruit characterized by a divided wall which consists of a fleshy outer layer derived from the flower receptacle and a leathery inner layer. The best-known representative is the apple, whose seeds are encased in a leathery envelope derived from the outer layer of the ovary wall. The shriveled remnants of sepals and stamens at the tip of the fruit are evidence that the apple is an accessory fruit. The core, the part thrown away, is derived from the ovary.

A multiple fruit is the product not of a single flower but of clusters of flowers whose ovaries grew tightly bunched together. Typical examples of trees that produce multiple fruits are the sycamore and the plane tree, with their "button balls" (see picture pages 50 and 147), the Osage orange, the mulberry, and the breadfruit tree.

How a tree functions

A tree grows simultaneously in two different ways: by adding new cells to already existing ones, and by increasing the size of already existing cells. In particular, this is what happens:

A new tree begins its life at the moment a male gamete fuses with an egg. Immediately on fertilization, the single-celled egg begins to divide into two identical cells which divide again, and again, and again, the cells gradually differentiating until a tiny embryo is produced. This embryo, which is only one-twenty-fifth of an inch in length or smaller, can be seen clearly when we split an acorn along its natural dividing line. Imbedded at the pointed end between the halves rests a minute spindle, exquisitely formed, pale yellow and smooth as if turned from old ivory—the embryo. Silently, quietly, it lies cradled between the two *cotyledons*, the seedling leaves of concentrated carbohydrates which will sustain the seedling tree until its first green leaves sprout and it become a self-sufficient, food-producing plant.

This tiny plant embryo does not look like much, but it is both marvel and mystery, this little speck of nothing, this future tree which could have grown into a mighty oak had our curiosity not interfered. Like any other seed, it is concentrated energy, dormant, waiting for the great moment of germination. Warm it, water it, and, though outwardly still immobile, it will begin to seethe with inner chemical activity, striving to fulfill the momentous plan that exists in its genes. This is the marvel: that from the union of two invisible specks of matter—two gametes—can come a tree, a giant, an oak which in turn will give rise to future oaks, and these again to others, and others still, always the same kind of tree, never failing, on and on indefinitely.

And this is the mystery: that, although much is known about the mechanics of this marvel—the shape, size, and chemical composition of the involved parts—the essence of this creative act still eludes us. Although we know fairly well what goes on, we still do not know why. We can mix all the proper chemicals and stir them and cook them and chill them and irradiate them and treat the mixture in every way known to science and our broth still remains sterile. All around us life creates itself in overwhelming profusion; it is as common as dust. But what life is we do not know. Nor how it began. Nor why it goes on. All we know is that it does exist, invincibly and forever.

Warmth and water activate a seed: warmth awakens the sleeping germ; water induces growth. The first stage of growth consists of a general enlargement of all the parts of the seed through an increase in turgor: by gorging themselves with water the cells distend, the seed swells and in swelling bursts its protective shell. Two probing sprouts appear, a tiny root that burrows downward and a fragile stem that pushes up. The two cotyledons expand, and the young tree is launched into the battle for light and life.

During the earliest stage in the life of a tree growth is achieved exclusively by an enlargement of already existing seed cells through swelling. However, once the initial burst is over this growth is no longer a three-dimensional increase in volume, but a two-dimensional elongation of root and stem during which the cells increase a hundredfold in length but very little, if at all, in thickness. The secret of this two-way stretch lies in the construction of the cell walls. They are like a rubber hose whose walls are reinforced by a metal spiral and thus stretchable lengthwise. The object of this one-way growth is to get the root down into the earth and the stem up into the light as fast as possible without wasting the food reserves. For not until it has unfurled its leaves is a tree able to produce food.

Soon, of course, a limit to growth through stretching is reached, and further increase in size requires the creation of new cells. Most of these are produced in special growth areas located at or near the tip of the new plant, and in older plants at and near the ends of twigs. First, cells multiply by division; then they stretch ten to twenty times in length, approximately doubling their size each day. After this, they harden into wood. From time to time, new cell groups push out sideways, forming the first beginnings of leaves. From the bases of leaves buds form that eventually grow into branches.

As the tree grows it increases in two dimensions: branches increase in length, and the trunk and branches increase in girth. But the actual zones where growth occurs remain limited: branches and roots grow in length only at their tips, and increases in thickness occur only within the *cambium*, the microscopically thin layer that lies between the bark and the wood. The rest of the tree—the woody parts, the *xylem*—can no longer grow; it has lost its ability to form new cells, and its old cells, like hardened arteries, can no longer stretch because their walls are stiff with *lignin;* they have turned to wood. For a while this woody portion—the sapwood—continues to conduct water and sap while also storing food. But as the cambium moves outward with increasing age and girth the cells of the living sapwood gradually clog up with gum and other substances, giving it a darker color; it becomes heartwood and dies. So a tree can be dead at its heart while its twigs are still in the prime of youth and its flowers at the height of vigor.

Because of this final hardening of its structural cells into wood, a tree grows taller and its crown spreads, from only the last few inches of its twigs. The rest—the woody skeleton—remains at a standstill. The monogrammed heart which lovers carve into its bark will not move upward as the tree grows older. The only sign of growth in trunk and limbs are increases in girth.

Although both grow by cell division, animals and trees grow in accordance with different rules. Animal growth follows a much more rigid plan than tree growth: once an animal has reached maturity, it ceases to grow; a tree grows until it dies. Even when a tree has reached the stage where mechanical strains put an end to further growth in height, it continues to increase in girth, each year adding a new layer to the circumference of trunk and branches. Furthermore, an animal's design is much more rigid than a tree's: every dog has four legs, every bird two wings, every mouse one tail; but no such plan determines the number of branches of an oak. An animal's design is based on symmetry—radial symmetry for many of the lower animals, bilateral symmetry for higher animals and man. But although each species of tree follows a definite scheme which provides its character, variations within the frame of this scheme are enormous; among all the oaks in the world no two are exactly alike. If a man loses an arm, he is crippled for life; if a tree loses a branch, the wound will heal, tissue and bark will cover it in time. As a matter of fact, so great is the regenerative power of some trees that whole new trees can be grown from cuttings. Nurserymen usually raise willows, poplars, and some other trees by simply sticking twigs into the ground. Given the proper care, such cuttings will develop roots and become big trees. This way of propagation occurs even in nature: a freshly broken willow branch may float downstream, drift into a quiet cove, become partly buried in the mud, and grow into a new tree. Years ago, one of my old apple trees was struck down in a storm and died. But near the top of its prostrate shattered trunk little rootlets formed, and from this point once near the very top of the tree green shoots sprouted. As the parent log slowly sank into the grassy ground these shoots kept on growing, lustily and tall, and became a new apple tree which today is some twenty feet high.

To be able to grow and reproduce itself, a tree, like any living organism, needs food. But unlike an animal, which depends on food produced by others, a tree—like any green plant—is able to produce its own food from raw chemicals taken directly from the air and the ground. These raw materials are primarily carbon dioxide and water which the tree, using sunlight for energy, converts into sugar, giving off oxygen as a by product. This process of photosynthesis is, as we have seen, carried on in the leaves. We will learn more about this fascinating and vitally important operation in Chapter IX.

In order to carry on photosynthesis and digest the food it has produced a tree requires large amounts of water. This water is taken from the ground by the roots and transported all the way up to the leaves through a vast and intricate circulation system that has its beginning in the millions of fine root hairs and ends in the leaves. How a tree is able to transport this water and raise it to the height of its crown until recently has been a mystery. To appreciate this tremendous feat, know that to lift water to the top of a 360-foot redwood tree a pressure of about 420 pounds per square inch at the root is required. However, at sea level, atmospheric pressure is only about fifteen pounds per square inch, sufficient to lift water by suction only some thirty-three feet. Hence, the old assumption according to which the leaves drew water from the roots by simple suction is obviously wrong. Then it was thought that water rose within the fine vascular pipelines of a tree by capillary action—drawn upward by the same force that makes liquid rise within a fine tube and causes blotting paper to absorb ink. However, this hypothesis was abandoned when experiment proved that water could be lifted only a few feet in this way. A new explanation may be that forces acting in the leaves draw water up through the tree. This process begins to operate when *transpiration*—loss of water from leaf tissues through evaporation under the influence of solar radiation—creates a water deficiency within the leaf cells. The drying cells, in a complex chemical reaction involving both *imbibition*—water absorption by the colloidal cell plasma—and *osmosis*—the diffusion of water through the differentially permeable cell walls—draw water from neighboring, still saturated cells. These, being depleted of their water content, in turn deplete adjacent cells, and so on all the way through the leaf stalk and the branches and trunk into the roots. Thus, continuous fine unbroken columns of water extend all the way from the leaf into the soil. That these columns do not pull apart under their own weight is due to the forces of *cohesion*—the intermolecular attraction that makes water particles stick to one another. Experiments have shown that under certain conditions—for example, when water is confined to very thin tubes such as those that constitute the conductive tissues of a tree—the forces of cohesion are so strong that a pull of 5,000 pounds per square inch is required to tear such a water column apart. In other words, under conditions such as found in the interior of trees, water possesses a tensile strength equivalent to 200 atmospheres, but forces equivalent to only ten to fifteen atmospheres of pressure are required to send water up into the crown of the tallest tree. So the mystery of how a tree the height of a thirty-five-story skyscraper is able to pump water all the way up to its top seems at last to have been solved.

The sum total of chemical processes necessary to keep living organisms alive and functioning is *metabolism*. As far as trees are concerned, metabolism involves two main processes: *photosynthesis* and *respiration*. Photosynthesis, a constructive or *anabolic* process, produces the food on which the tree lives. Respiration, a destructive or *catabolic* process, breaks down the food produced by the tree in order to release the energy which all living organisms require to power their life processes.

It may seem that a tree—an apparently passive and inert organism—would require very little energy, but nothing could be further from the truth. Energy is needed to power a number of different processes all vitally important to the welfare of a tree. Foremost of these is *assimilation*—by which food is broken down or *digested* and reassembled in different form to become the substance of the tree: protoplasm, cell walls, and wood; trunk, branches, leaves, and flowers; fruits and seeds; and so on. Energy is also used up in the constant streaming of protoplasm within the cells; in cell division and the movements of chromosomes; in the processes by which nutrients from the soil are accumulated by the roots; and in the synthesis of enzymes, hormones, vitamins, pigments, and other substances—such as organic acids, alkaloids, tannins, oils, resins, and gums that are necessary to the functioning of a tree.

A comparison between photosynthesis and respiration shows that they are chemically opposite. In photosynthesis carbon dioxide is used and oxygen released; in respiration oxygen is used and carbon dioxide released. Photosynthesis goes on only in the presence of light; respiration takes place continuously day and night as long as the tree is alive. Photosynthesis occurs at a much higher rate than respiration, with the result that a tree releases far more oxygen than it consumes and takes up more carbon dioxide from the air than it gives off. Actually, the amount of carbon dioxide given off in respiration is so small that it is completely unnecessary to remove plants from bedrooms during the night as is frequently done, particularly in hospitals, in the belief that the liberated carbon dioxide is harmful to the health. Careful measurements of the carbon dioxide in the air in greenhouses early in the morning has shown that the concentration of this gas averaged only about .05 per cent. It is known that concentrations of up to .6 per cent of carbon dioxide produce no harmful effects in man.

Respiration is a burning process since it involves oxidation; the reaction of oxygen with the carbon and hydrogen molecules of the plant sugars (produced by photosynthesis) form water and carbon dioxide, thereby releasing energy. In this respect a tree can be likened to a machine, for instance, an internal combustion engine which burns (i.e., oxidizes) gasoline and through this process of combustion produces energy—the horsepower that drives the car. Only, in the case of the automobile engine the oxidation process is rather violent and fast, whereas plant respiration occurs at a much slower and less violent rate. Animals also respire, although animal respiration must not be confused with breathing. All animals respire, but only certain animals (including man) breathe. Respiration—an indispensible requirement

for the maintenance of any kind of life—is the process by which gases are exchanged between the atmosphere and the internal tissues of the living body, no matter whether animal or plant, whereas breathing designates merely the operation of the mechanical apparatus by means of which outside air is conducted to an exchange surface, specifically the lungs, and air containing a higher content of water vapor and carbon dioxide is expelled.

The senses of trees

Whether or not trees can "feel" depends on our definition of the term. If we mean feelings of the kind that depend on consciousness, such as happiness or pain, then science answers with an unqualified no. But if we mean sensitivity and reaction to outside stimuli, the answer is affirmative. How do we know? Feeling based on consciousness and emotion presupposes the existence of a nervous system and a brain; trees, in common with all plants, lack both. Therefore, they cannot possibly have "feelings." On the other hand, that trees are sensitive to certain outside stimuli is obvious to anyone who has ever touched a mimosa leaf and seen it fold its leaflets in response or watched a sunflower slowly turn its head with the sun. But is there really a basic difference between emotional awareness and mechanical response, or is it only a matter of degree?

Botanists say that the difference is fundamental; trees do not feel; they cannot be aware because they have no brain, no consciousness. Yet if I watch a patch of snow melt under the stimulus of solar heat I know this reaction is purely physical: the snow crystals respond predictably in accordance with basic natural laws. But when I look through a microscope and watch a unicellular flagellate—one of the most primitive of all living plants—as it responds to light in accordance with information received by its eyespot, I am no longer sure whether the reaction of this one-celled organism is as mechanical and "unfeeling" as the melting of the snow. Is something else involved, something less deterministic, more the result of choice than that of cause and effect? Could the response of living matter be subject to laws so far unknown, or unknowable?

However, be this as it may, it is a fact that trees possess specific senses: they are able to respond to gravity, contact, shock, temperature, and light. They also seem to have a sense of time.

In order to live, a germinating seedling must sink its root into the soil for anchorage and water and raise its stem toward the light. This presupposes a sense of direction, a response to gravity which scientifically is called *geotropism*. Geotropism occurs in two forms: *positive* geotropism to which the root responds by growing downward; and *negative* geotropism, which causes the stem to grow upward. That geotropism is a true sense of gravity and not perhaps the effect of moisture or light upon the germinating seedling (or, for that matter, the mature tree) has been conclusively established by experiment: if we place, say, an acorn inside a narrow horizontal tube and let it germinate in total darkness, both its root and stem will, of course, grow horizontally as long as they are confined by the tube. But as soon as they reach its end, the root will abruptly bend downward and the stem upward. However, if we now plant this same seedling tree in a little pot fastened to the rim of a turntable and spin the turntable rapidly, the root will change direction and grow horizontally outward, while the stem will bend toward the hub of the wheel and grow horizontally inward. This change of direction is caused by the centrifugal force which now is stronger than gravity although, in principle, it represents the same gravitational pull exerted in a different direction.

The controlling factor which regulates these plant movements is the growth hormone, *auxin*. Auxins seem to have four main properties, some of which are rather perplexing and still not fully understood. They are relatively heavy and therefore tend to collect along the lower side of horizontal or leaning stems or roots; they can move in only one direction within the body of the plant—away from the tip of the stem or the root where they are produced—even if this means moving against gravity; in a trunk or branch a high concentration of auxin stimulates growth, but in a root a high concentration has the opposite effect and inhibits growth; and, finally, auxins are negatively light sensitive, which means that they tend to move toward the shaded side of a trunk or branch (why this should be is not known). The mechanism of geotropic plant growth seems to function as follows: in a leaning or horizontally placed stem gravity causes auxin to collect in greater concentration on its lower than on its upper side; as a result the cells on the lower side grow and multiply faster than the cells on the upper side so that the stem bends upward. Exactly the opposite is assumed to happen in regard to the root: the greater concentration of auxin on the lower side of the root seems to inhibit cell growth with the result that a higher rate of growth on the upper side causes the root to bend downward. But there are many perplexing exceptions. For example, the lower branches of pin oak grow downward, and many root systems extend primarily in the horizontal plane. The mechanics of directional growth are still far from being understood.

Plant sensitivity to light is well known. Stems and leaves grow and turn toward the light; roots either do not respond to light at all or shy away from it. The response to light—*phototropism*—is positive if the response is growth toward the light, negative if it is growth away from the light.

Like geotropism, phototropism is induced by auxins. In this case, it is the negative light sensitivity of these growth hormones which cause a plant to bend toward the light. The branches of a tree standing at the edge of a wood, for example, which receive light mainly from one direction, will grow toward the light because there will be a concentration of auxins on the shaded side of the branch.

Trunk and branches generally (there are many exceptions) grow in the direction of the greatest concentration of light, but leaves commonly react to light so that their upper surfaces face it at an angle of approximately 90 degrees. Since each leaf orients itself to receive a maximum share of light and avoids being shaded by the neighboring leaves, the result is an arrangement—a *leaf mosaic*—which largely minimizes the inevitable overlapping and presents a maximum exposure of combined leaf surface to the light.

Many plants are sensitive to contact and touch. In this respect, two kinds of reaction can be distinguished: *thigmotropism* and *thigmonasty*. Thigmotropism is growth in response to contact with a solid object, with the direction of the response being determined by the stimulus. A good example is the strangler fig (see picture pages 110 and 111) which on contact with the trunk of its victim encircles it in a tight and murderous web, probably as the result of an increase in the rate of cell growth on the side opposite the stimulating contact. Other examples of thigmotropism are the tight coiling of tendrils of vines around their supports. Thigmonasty is movement in response to touch, but in this case, the direction of the movement is independent of that of the stimulus. Well-known examples are the folding of the leaves of the mimosa plant and the closing of the leaf trap of the Venus'-flytrap. In both cases, changes in hydraulic pressure within specific cells—changes in *turgor*—set off intricate and complex trigger mechanisms, resulting in movement.

Still other tree senses register acidity or alkalinity, moisture, temperature, and even time. For example, all the winter buds on a given tree open on the same day, and it makes no difference that some grow on low, shaded branches or facing north while others are fully exposed to warmth and light; they still open together. All the apple trees in an orchard flower simultaneously. The signals which make buds or trees act synchronously are only partially understood. Some, of course, such as those that make all the leaves of a tree come out together, must be internal. Others are external and probably connected with the degree and duration of the cold to which a tree has been exposed during the winter, the length of day and night, and the temperatures of spring. However, much in the field of plant growth and responses is still conjecture, and our knowledge has many blank spots. But uncertainty and ignorance only make the study of trees all the more fascinating—a challenge to imaginative experiments. Each discovery brings us closer to an understanding of the great mystery of life.

Picture pages 37–51

37. Ginkgo, or maidenhair tree *(Ginkgo biloba)*. This magnificent specimen, which stands on the grounds of the Vanderbilt Estate in Hyde Park, New York, repeats in its growth pattern the triangular theme of its leaves. Together with the palm-like cycads, the ginkgo is the most primitive naked-seed plant living today—its ancient lineage goes back some 230 million years to Permian times. It is a "living fossil"—and looks it. Palms, joshua, and boojum "trees" excepted, no other tree appears so primitive as a ginkgo, so gawky and crude; it seems a prototype tree, the result of a tentative and not quite successful design for a new kind of plant. Its leaves, too, are unlike those of any other tree, strange and primitive, dichotomously veined, triangular, leathery, broadly

fanshaped and usually divided by a deep indentation into two more or less symmetrical halves—a clue to instant recognition.

38. Blue gum, commonly called eucalyptus *(Eucalyptus globulus)*. Eucalyptus, an Australian import, is now one of the most common trees in California. It is easily recognized by its shredded bark that peels off in long, narrow strips, exposing pastel-colored patches of underbark that give the trunk a shaggy appearance. The narrow, tough leaves have an aromatic fragrance when crushed. Since the leaves fall at irregular intervals, the eucalyptus gives the impression of being an evergreen.

39. Spruce forest in Denmark. These trees represent typical examples of excurrent growth—a pattern characterized by a single shaft-like trunk with relatively small lateral branches arranged in whorls which can be seen with particular clarity in the fallen tree.

40. Royal palm *(Roystonea regia)*. This magnificent, strictly tropical palm, which can reach a height of 100 feet, is native to south Florida and Cuba. It can be spotted instantly among other palms by its relatively smooth, gray-white trunk (see also picture page 57) which resembles a column of poured concrete. Bulbous and swollen at the base, it is topped by a smooth, green, glossy, six- to ten-foot section of sheath-like leaf bases which are part of the current growth of feathery twelve- to fifteen-foot fronds.

41. American beech *(Fagus grandifolia)*. This tree is easily identified by its generally smooth, sometimes wrinkled but never cracked or furrowed, silver-gray bark which looks like cast aluminum (see also picture pages 72 and 134–135). The only other North American tree with similar bark is the American hornbeam, or blue beech *(Carpinus caroliniana)*. However, this relatively small tree never reaches the dimensions of an American beech, and its trunk and main branches have an unusual sculptured and quasi-"muscular" appearance unlike the essentially cylindrical American beech.

42. Long-leaf pine *(Pinus palustris)*. The identifying feature of this southern pine is its enormous needles which grow up to eighteen inches long in clusters

of three—the longest needles of any pine in the world. This is the most valuable timber pine of the South and, because stands have been lumbered heavily, large specimens of this beautiful tree, which may grow to a height of eighty-five feet, are rare nowadays.

43. White pine *(Pinus strobus)*. This is the only American pine whose two- to four-inch needles are grouped in bundles of five—an infallible clue to its identity. White pine is the most important timber tree in the Northeast. It is—or rather was, because few if any of these giants have survived the lumberman's ax —also one of the tallest, with old specimens growing up to 220 feet. Boards thirty-six inches wide and wider can still be found in the flooring or paneling of old colonial homes in New England, testifying to the enormous size of these vanished trees.

44. White ash *(Fraxinus americana)*. This is the largest, most common, and commercially most valuable of all American ashes. Its wood is prized for its hardness, toughness, and strength and therefore it is used primarily for such items as ax and tool handles, oars, baseball bats, tennis rackets, skis, wagon wheels, agricultural implements, and furniture. Ashes are the only American trees that have pinnately compound leaves which come in pairs, i.e., two leafstalks opposite each other on the branch, each bearing from five to eleven leaflets depending on the species, a sure clue to identification.

45. Sycamore *(Platanus occidentalis)*. No other tree of the Eastern United States grows so massive as a sycamore, the largest specimens having trunks with diameters of twelve to fourteen feet. This tree is instantly recognizable by its bark, which flakes off cleanly in irregularly curved, jigsaw puzzle-like pieces, exposing the whitish underbark. The rough, white, hard-to-split wood is prized for butchers' blocks. The leaves (see picture page 84) resemble those of maple, but are larger and thicker, with shallower lobes. The ball-shaped fruit dangling on thin stalks (see picture page 50) provides another unmistakable clue to the identity of this tree.

46. Tulip tree, or yellow poplar *(Liriodendron tulipifera)*. This is one of the tallest Eastern forest trees, characterized by a trunk that rises arrow-straight in columnar splendor before the first lateral branches appear. The diamond-patterned bark is deeply furrowed. The straight-grained, white, rather soft and easily worked wood is used for hat blocks since it does not warp and swell when exposed to live steam. Tulip trees never form pure stands, but grow singly among other forest trees—hemlock, maple, hickory, oak, etc. They can be spotted by the straightness of their trunks. But the most infallible clue to their identity is the unique shape of the leaf (see pictures pages 88–89), which, unlike the leaf of any other tree, is notched at the tip.

47. European willow *(Salix sp.)*. To induce the growth of masses of long thin shoots for use in making baskets, this tree has been *pollarded*, i.e., its branches have been repeatedly cut back to the trunk. I found it standing by the side of a road in central France, where basket-making is a native industry and pollarded trees a familiar sight.

48–49. White oak *(Quercus alba)*. The difference in growth pattern between two trees of the same species, one of which grew up in the open and the other among trees, is clearly shown in these pictures. At the left, the open-grown tree has a short, squat trunk supporting massive horizontal limbs. At the right, the bole of the forest-grown tree is thinner and taller, raising its crown above the canopy formed by lesser trees nearby. Despite these differences in growth, the character— the "personality"—of both trees is identical; the gnarled boughs and twisted branches as well as the over-all impression of toughness and strength unmistakably spell "white oak."

50. Sycamore fruit *(Platanus occidentalis)*. Also called "button balls," these dangling one-inch spheres look like notes of music in the sky. Since there is only one sphere at the end of each stalk, this tree is an American sycamore; if there were two, it would be a London plane tree *(Platanus acerifolia)*. Each ball contains a large number of tiny, very hairy seeds.

51. Sausage-tree fruit *(Kigelia pinnata)*. This unusual African import is planted in various parts of southern Florida as a tourist attraction. It presents a remarkable sight, its inedible, eighteen-inch-long, gourd-like fruits dangling singly or in clusters of two and more from three-foot stalks.

VI
Live Oaks

If I had to choose the "tree of trees"—the most beautiful, majestic, yet "friendliest" of all trees, the tree which as far as humans are concerned is the most rewarding, not in terms of lumber and cash, but in the creation of an atmosphere of comfort, well-being, and peace—I would choose the live oak. No other tree combines more virtues with fewer faults. Some trees, such as the redwood and sequoia, overwhelm with their enormousness—their scale is superhuman; they inspire awe rather than love; the feelings they evoke are as remote as the places where they grow. Others, such as the bristlecone pine, are fascinating and unique, but are neither particularly beautiful nor utilitarian. Pine, spruce, and fir may be the most useful of all trees, but they are often rather dull. Horse-chestnut, flowering dogwood, and magnolia have lovely flowers and are very beautiful temporarily, but they lack distinction and strength. Northern oaks have great strength but no "warmth." Apple, cherry, and peach trees are warm and pretty when in bloom but otherwise bland. Palms are occasionally romantic. Beeches and birches are heartbreakingly lovely in spring, but they lose this quality by summer. But live oaks are perfect all year round.

Of all the trees of the American South, the live oak seems to me the most typical, the "picture postcard tree." Its very name evokes images of hot sun and cool shade, gracious living, mint juleps, and columned *ante bellum* mansions, slowly decaying among tall weeds overshadowed by century-old live oaks whose reaching branches are gray and heavy with festoons of Spanish moss. In a hot country where shade is one of the necessities of life, no trees fulfill this purpose more perfectly than live oaks. Not tall as trees go—they rarely exceed sixty-five feet—live oaks easily spread twice as far as their height. Their massive limbs are often thicker than the trunks of other good-sized trees, immense arches rising in high parabolas and returning to earth again sixty and more feet from the trunk or else stretching horizontally for greater distances than the boughs of any other tree. The shadow which a century-old live oak casts is immense and neither excessively dense nor sparse. Light and air pass freely through the interstices between the leaves and create a feeling not unlike that of being in a room the doors and windows of which are louvered to let in light and air while shutting out glare and heat. Four hundred people or three dozen cars fit comfortably in the space shaded by a single oak.

Deeply grooved and ridged bark protects the trunk and the main branches, which often are embellished with rows of graceful little ferns whose tiny roots find soil and minerals in moss-grown fissures. The leaves are small and narrow, rounded, leathery, and thick. Live oaks are evergreens; hence their name. Unlike deciduous trees which appear "dead" in winter, live oaks keep their old leaves until new ones take over the task of manufacturing food for the tree. In this respect live oaks differ from northern oaks, which are deciduous trees whose ancestors emigrated from the South, where they had been evergreens. Remnants of this evergreen tradition still linger in the habit of most northern oaks of holding on to their dead leaves through the winter. Other deciduous trees form each fall a brittle little plate at the junction of leaf stem and twig which enables the leaf to break off cleanly. In northern oaks, however, and particularly in younger trees, this shearing device often fails to form, with the result that the leaves, though brown and dead, may stay on the tree till spring.

Live oaks are found south from Virginia all along the Atlantic Coast, on offshore islands to Biscayne Bay in Florida, and along the Gulf Coast westward to the Rio Grande. In past times their wood was highly prized by shipwrights. Their strength and toughness made them particularly suitable for fashioning keels and ribs which were assembled from timber that had grown in the required shapes—angular or curved as the case may have been. Nowadays, live oak wood fortunately has little commercial value—trunks are too short to be sawn into lumber of sufficiently useful length, and in the South the need for firewood is small. Today, live oaks are valued primarily for their beauty and their shade, so most Southern communities take great pride in these magnificent trees and see to it that they are properly protected.

Yet on my last big trip in search of pictures for this book I found one example, not of misuse but of nonuse, which saddened me; this was the plight of the tree known as "Florida's Treaty Oak" in Jacksonville, Florida. Granted, this magnificent century-old oak with almost the widest span I have ever seen was protected by a strong, high, wire mesh fence. But it was standing in a part of Jacksonville that can only be called a slum, amidst run-down garages, abandoned shacks, and back lots littered with junk. It is admittedly difficult to protect a tree adequately from climbing children and youthful vandals when its immense horizontal branches curve back far enough nearly to touch the ground. Yet it seems to me that some way could be found for this spectacular tree to be made the center of a little park where children could play and people rest in its shade. And by emphasizing its historic past, this live oak could easily become an attraction that would draw additional visitors to Jacksonville.

Picture pages 52–56

Moss-covered live oaks near Charleston, South Carolina. Although the live oak is one of the commonest trees in the South and beautiful specimens abound even in back yards, along country roads, and particularly in old rural cemeteries, the most majestic trees are generally found on the grounds of old estates and plantations, most of which are nowadays open to visitors. The trees shown in these photographs grace the entrance avenue of Middleton Gardens, just outside Charleston, and represent some of the finest examples of live oak I have ever seen. In early spring, when the camellias are in bloom, this magnificent old private park is open to the public and a visit is well worth the nominal entrance fee. Bounded on one side by a highly picturesque country road lined with arching moss-hung live oaks and on the other by the grassy banks of the Charleston River, this beautiful estate is a veritable botanical garden where open spaces alternate with jungle-like thickets and somber old oaks are set off effectively by the burning colors of the smaller camellia trees that border the moss-grown winding paths.

Live oaks seem to me incomplete without their swaying garlands of "Spanish moss"—they seem to be hung with Biblical beards. Spanish moss is not "Spanish" nor a true moss nor a parasite; it is a so-called air plant, an *epiphyte*, which grows on other plants (or, for that matter, on telephone wires) without having any structural involvement with them or taking anything from them. Spanish moss manufactures its own food from dust particles, air, rainwater, and dew, which it absorbs through the minute scales that cover its leaves and stems. Several times, I have brought home from a trip to the South a handful of Spanish moss which I "planted" on a wire strung in my bathroom, where it lived happily for years and even produced minute flowers. Many visitors to the South at first find Spanish moss repulsive. But after a while they usually succumb to its spell and realize how well it suits the landscape and the trees, the hot sun and the cool shade. Swaying slowly in the gentle summer breeze, fiercely independent, Spanish moss somehow manages to express something of the essence of the American South.

64

VII
Trunk and Bark

The massive trunk of a majestic tree is a structure as functional, characteristic, and beautiful as any classical column. As the function of a column is to hold up the roof, so the function of the trunk is to hold high the crown of a tree so that its leaves may receive the best exposure to light and air. But whereas most columns have but a single purpose—to serve as vertical supports—a trunk fulfills additional functions. It provides a "backbone" for the tree that is both stiff and elastic, enabling it to weather all but the most destructive storms; it furnishes a suitable base for branches; it houses a marvelous transportation system to convey water and nutrients from the roots to the leaves and distribute food manufactured by the leaves throughout the entire tree; it furnishes its own protection; and it is "functional" to such an extent that it even adjusts itself to the ever-mounting load of the growing crown and the expanding needs of the tree by steadily increasing in girth.

Similar to the way that, for example, a Doric column is different from an Ionic or a Corinthian column, the trunk of a beech differs from that of an ash, birch, sycamore, or any other tree. In most cases, its characteristics are not even subtle or obscure as might be believed by those people to whom a beech, ash, birch, or sycamore is merely "a tree." They are most often so distinct that they can serve as means of identification, as the following pictures will demonstrate.

Finally, a tree trunk is a thing of beauty. Its size and massiveness, its form and configuration, its texture—all are qualities that appeal strongly to any sensitive eye, stimulate the inquisitive mind, and provide food for the imagination. The more familiar we become with different kinds of trees and the more we observe and learn about them, the greater our enjoyment and satisfaction. And eventually, imperceptibly, trees will "come to life."

The best way of studying the structural organization of a tree trunk is to examine the stump of a recently cut tree. All its elements are arranged in a more or less concentric pattern. In particular, the following components must be distinguished:

The pith is the tissue which, like a spinal cord, occupies the center of the trunk and every branch and twig. It normally consists of simple unspecialized cells which die after a number of years and decompose, so that in old trunks the pith usually exists merely as a void. The organization of these cells is not always uniform and therefore can provide clues for the identification of certain kinds of trees. This is best done by slicing a twig lengthwise with a sharp knife or razor blade to expose the pith. Although in the majority of trees the pith appears homogenous, in others it is differentially organized. The pith of the tulip tree, for example, is not uniform but *diaphragmed*, i.e., marked at intervals by narrow bands of darker tissue. In other trees, such as black walnut, black gum, butternut, and Paulownia, the pith is *chambered*, i.e., hollow except for narrow transverse partitions. In still others it is not firm but *spongy* as in the twigs of the wahoo of Arkansas and the spindle tree. In cross section the pith may be either *circular* (the most common form found, among others, in the elms), *triangular* (as in the alders), or *star-sheaped*, five-angled (as in the aspens, poplars, hickories, and oaks). Even the color of the pith can be significant. For example, it is white in the common elder, but salmon-colored in the red elder, buff-colored in black walnut, and chocolate brown in the twigs of butternut.

The wood, of course, comprises the largest part of the trunk. It surrounds the pith in thin, more or less concentric and circular layers which on the surface of the stump appear in rings, each ring normally representing one year's growth. The number of these rings—the *annual growth rings* of the tree—counted close to the ground, is therefore, as a rule (there are exceptions), a good indicator of the age of the tree. On the other hand, most tropical trees—for example, mahogany—lack well-defined annual rings because the even climate extends the growing season throughout the entire year.
Usually, the inner core of the wood is darker than the outer layers, the difference in color being particularly striking in red cedar, black walnut, and redwood; in other trees, however, notably poplar, basswood, and

spruce, this color difference is less pronounced and may even be absent. This inner, darker part is called the *heartwood*. It consists of cells that have died and clogged with organic compounds. The outer, lighter layer of wood is called the *sapwood* and consists of live cells that still function as conductors of water and sap although they are unable to grow or multiply. Whereas the sapwood is vitally necessary to the survival of a tree, the only remaining function of the heartwood (which, of course, once was sapwood) is to strengthen the trunk. Actually, a tree can live and function without its heartwood, a fact testified to by the large number of hollow apple trees, maples, redwoods, and others whose heartwood has long since decayed or been eaten out by fire. The only adverse effect of this hollowness is that such empty shells have less resistance to breakage than solid trunks. More detailed information on wood is given in Chapter XIII.

The cambium is the microscopically thin layer beneath the bark which, like an extremely fine skin, envelops the entire sapwood of a tree—roots, trunk, branches, and twigs. It is within this layer that all the lateral growth of a tree takes place: toward the inside of the trunk or branch the cambium produces the new cells that form the annual growth rings of *xylem*, or wood, and in so doing pushes itself outward; toward the outside it forms new cells that add to the thickness of the *phloem*.

The phloem, the layer immediately outside the cambium, makes up the inner portion of the bark. It consists primarily of *sieve tubes* and *vascular rays*—conductive tissues which play an important role in the movement of food throughout the tree. If this movement, most of which takes place vertically, is interrupted by girdling the tree—i.e., removing a ring-shaped section of the bark right down to the wood—the tree dies. If a tree is girdled early in the growing season, a curious phenomenon often happens: the part of the trunk above the girdle increases in girth while the one below remains the same. This abnormal enlargement is caused by a "traffic jam" in the movement of tree-manufactured food which on its way from the leaves to the root cannot pass the girdled section and is therefore available for abnormal growth. Such a girdled tree may survive temporarily, but must sooner or later perish because its roots will literally starve to death and cease to ab-

sorb water, causing the dehydrated leaves to wilt and die.

The bark forms the outermost layer of trunk, branches, and twigs. In saplings and twigs it consists of only the *epidermis*, a single layer of protective cells, and usually appears green because it is so thin that the underlying chlorophyll shows through. As the tree grows older, the bark gains several layers: dead cells of phloem on the inside; a layer called the *cortex* which serves as a storehouse for food; and the *cork cambium* which produces the outermost layer of bark, *cork*. Cork is an excellent insulator which effectively protects the delicate cambium from sudden thermal changes. It also heals injured stem tissues by forming a protective layer which keeps out decay fungi and prevents dehydration. Eventually, the outer layers of cork cells die with age, and, since dead tissues cannot grow and adjust to increases in girth of trunk and branches, the bark develops fissures and cracks as the expanding wood presses from within. In certain trees, however, such as beech, birch, some cherries, and many tropical trees, the outer layer of bark does not die, and its cells continue to divide. As a result, the bark does not crack, but expands as trunk and branches increase in girth and, though it may wrinkle (see picture pages 72, 134, and 135), stays relatively smooth.
Since the bark of most trees is as characteristic as their leaves, it is an important aid in identification. The following photographs are intended to show how different and beautiful bark can be.

Picture pages 57–75

57. Royal palm *(Roystonea regia)*. These most stately of palms are easily recognized by their light gray trunks which look as if they were cast of poured concrete. Even the horizontal ridges seem to be faithful reproductions of concrete that has penetrated into the joints between the forms.

58. Bald cypress *(Taxodium distichum)*. Together with live oak, this relative of redwood is the tree most typical of the Old South. Identifying features are its common location in the shallows of lakes, the deadwater of rivers, or on marshy, waterlogged ground; the flaring-buttressed base of the trunk; and the numer-

ous "knees" or breathing roots that rise above the water level between the trees like little round stumps. Since cypress is one of the most valuable lumber trees, old stands have been unmercifully decimated, and fully grown trees are extremely rare.

59.   Boojum tree *(Idria columnaris)*. Few plants are as weird and fantastic as these inhabitants of the deserts of Baja California, which look more like immense, up-side-down carrots than trees. Because they occur only in territory that is virtually inaccessible, little is known about them. These young specimens, whose trunk covering seems more like elephant hide than bark, are transplants that were photographed in the Botanical Garden of the Arizona-Sonora Desert Museum outside Tucson in a setting of paloverde trees and saguaro cacti.

60.   Madroña *(Arbutus menziesii)*. This is one of the most colorful trees of the Pacific Coast, recognizable by its dark green, gray, and deep brown mottled bark that flakes off easily in big scales, exposing large patches of suede-smooth, terracotta-colored underbark. Leaves are leathery and shiny, dark green above and whitish below, shaped like those of rhododendron. Trunks are usually leaning, branches thick and curving like frantically waving arms.

61.   Sweet cherry *(Prunus avium)*. The decorative, glossy, red-brown bark broken up by rough black horizontal stripes will help identify this tree.

62.   White oak *(Quercus alba;* see also picture pages 48–49)*.

63.   Chestnut oak *(Quercus montana)*.
Notice the differences in the bark of these two closely related trees of the white oak group. White oak has the lightest bark of all oaks. Chestnut oak bark is characterized by deep furrows which form a pattern of strongly elongated rectangular plates. For fair comparison, trees of approximately equal trunk diameters are reproduced here in identical scale.

64.   Gray birch *(Betula populifolia)*. Bark is chalky white and nonpeeling. Also typical (though not shown here) are conspicuous, triangular, black marks, the scars left by shed limbs.

65.   Sweet birch *(Betula lenta)*. The bark of young trees such as this one is smooth, glossy, dark reddish-brown, interrupted by the whitish lines of the *lenticels*, which provide aeration. The bark of old trees, however, is different—no longer smooth and shiny, but coarse and dull, consisting of large thick plates and heavy ridges which give the trunk an armor-plated appearance.

66.   Yellow birch *(Betula lutea)*. A means to instant identification are the masses of small gray and yellow curls of the bark which from a distance give the trunk an almost metallic appearance.

67.   Paper birch *(Betula papyrifera)*. Outwardly similar to gray birch except that the bark peels off naturally in wide, paper-thin strips which are chalk-white on the outside and golden brown inside. This is the tree from which vandals like to strip pieces of bark as "souvenirs." Once stripped, white bark will never grow again, and the injured place eventually will be covered with blackish scar tissue.

68.   Young shagbark hickory *(Carya ovata)*.

69.   Mature shagbark hickory *(Carya ovata)*. As in many other trees, the bark of young and old specimens differs. The trunk of a young hickory is covered with smooth, finely striped bark that gives a feeling of extreme hardness and solidity when touched. In contrast, the bark of an old hickory is scaly and peels off in rough, hard, curving strips that manage somehow to stay on the tree, providing an unmistakable clue to recognition.

70.   Hop hornbeam *(Ostrya virginiana)*. Gray, flaky, shredded-looking bark is typical of mature trees. And since the leaves are virtually identical with those of sweet birch (see picture page 65) which shares the same territory, it is the bark that provides a convenient means of distinguishing between the two. Another clue is the unique fruit of hop hornbeam, which consists of a small cluster of papery bags containing the seeds.

71.   Flowering dogwood *(Cornus florida)*. This is eastern America's most conspicuous flowering tree because the showy white blossoms normally break out

before its own leaves as well as those of most other trees. Compare its bark with that of hop hornbeam: from afar the trunks of both may look alike (although hop hornbeam grows into a much bigger tree), but closer inspection will reveal decisive differences—the outer bark of hop hornbeam consists of shredded peeling flakes, that of flowering dogwood of hard and firmly attached little plates. The tree observer must learn to distinguish small characteristics like these.

72. American beech *(Fagus grandifolia)*. The iron-gray, generally smooth and never deeply ridged or furrowed bark which looks as if it were tightly stretched over a hard cylindrical core is one of the best clues to the identity of beech, one of the stateliest of the North American forest trees.

73. White ash *(Fraxinus americana)*. The beautiful diamond pattern of the deeply furrowed bark is one of the characteristics of a mature ash. Another, shared by the ashes with the maples, dogwoods, buckeyes, and horse-chestnut, is the opposite arrangement of the leaves. But of all these trees the ashes alone have pinnately compound leaves.

74. California white oak *(Quercus lobata)*. A relative of the eastern white oak (see picture page 62), its bark is similar in design yet different in detail—its pattern tighter, its plates more sharply defined. The round-lobed leaves of this native of the Pacific Coast instantly reveal the tree as belonging to the white oak group.

75. Black locust *(Robinia pseudo-acacia;* see also picture page 31). Although superficially similar to the bark of white ash (see picture page 73), the bark of a mature black locust is still more deeply furrowed, its diamond pattern larger, its texture stringy instead of finely grained. This coarse, nearly black bark suits the gaunt and harsh frame of this powerful tree which, incongruously enough, produces delicate feathery compound leaves and clusters of lovely, fragrant white flowers.

61—69 ▶

73—75 ▶

VIII
The Tallest Living Things

The tallest tree on earth is a coast redwood. When it was measured in August 1966, a University of California survey team recorded its height at 369.2 feet—equal to a thirty-five-story skyscraper and more than twice the height of Niagara Falls. This champion of champions stands in the Founders' Grove in Humboldt Redwoods State Park in northern California, only a short distance from Highway 101. The photographs on picture pages 77–80 were made within half a mile of this tree. Each of the large redwoods shown in these pictures is 200 to 300 feet tall with a trunk diameter of eight to fifteen feet. Other record trees are a recently discovered 367.8-foot coast redwood located above Redwood Creek about ten miles east of the Pacific Ocean near Orick on Tree Farm land belonging to the Arcata Redwood Company; the 356.5-foot Rockefeller Tree in Humboldt Redwoods State Park fifty-eight miles farther south; and the 352.6-foot Founder's Tree that stands in Founder's Grove.

But it is not only their physical dimensions which make the coast redwoods unique. In sheer mass they are easily outstripped by their relatives, the giant sequoias (see picture pages 97–100) with trunks thirty feet in diameter. But sequoias are always intermixed with other, lesser trees or stand in small groups, whereas coast redwoods form large, virtually pure forests. Although many other kinds of trees also form pure forests (see picture pages 4, 5, 15, 39) these forests are different—they are just "woods." They do not possess the grandeur of a redwood forest, where trunks stand massive and arrow straight like pillars in a cathedral, their weathered bronze bark grooved and channeled, spiraling upward a hundred feet and more before the first branches appear, opening vistas of unrivaled magnificence.

Unfortunately, redwoods are commercially eminently desirable trees, and for over a hundred years a knockdown drag-out fight has been waged between the forces of commercialism, which want to cut these trees for wood and profit, and the forces of conserva-

tion, which want to preserve them. The lumber industry claims that its members pay substantial taxes and provide steady employment for a multitude of people; that the lumber it produces is urgently needed for industry; that 117,000 acres of coast redwood parks and groves have already been set aside in twenty-eight state parks and one national monument dedicated to perpetual preservation. To this the conservationists reply that there are still 1,576,000 acres of commercial timber-producing coast redwood forests in the Redwood region plus another 10,000 acres in Oregon; that, according to a 1964 study by Frank and Dean Solinsky, Inc., 62.5 per cent of the volume of all *virgin* redwood forests is privately owned and managed for lumber production; that some of the largest redwoods are still being cut; and that many of the existing "protected" redwood stands are not really protected because they are still endangered by periodic floods resulting from excessive deforestation of their watersheds.

That the last claim is particularly valid was recently demonstrated by the devastating flood of December 1964, when the waters of Bull Creek rose to an unprecedented height—thirty-five feet—and inundated Highway 101 near Weott in the heart of Humboldt Redwoods State Park. There can be no doubt that the main cause of this disaster was the ruthless deforestation of the upper slopes of Bull Creek Basin, where loggers had stripped steep slopes, gutted canyons, and gouged the hills with skid trails and roads. Several forest fires completed the devastation. Robbed of its protected trees, the basically unstable soil of the watershed easily washed away. By the winter of 1955–1956, Bull Creek, fed by abnormally heavy rains that ran off the barren slopes unrestrained and washed tons of silt and rubble into the creek, had cut a swath of destruction through the park and within a few hours had undercut and toppled 300 major trees. In this single disaster, 420 full-grown redwoods fell, ninety-eight had to be cut down because they were too far undercut by the flood to be saved, and some fifty acres of land were washed away.

When I visited this area a year and a half after the flood of 1964, the forest was almost devoid of undergrowth. Gone were most of the smaller trees and almost all the shrubs, ferns, and low plants that had formed the base from which the towering redwoods rose, their green foliage now replaced by gray mud and silt that, like a noxious coat of paint, covered the forest floor and the trunks of all the trees to a height of thirty feet. Both Bull Creek and the south fork of the Eel River had considerably broadened their channels and formed cutbanks with practically vertical slopes twenty feet high, dangerously under-cutting innumerable trees growing near their edges. Others, including some very large redwoods, had been uprooted by the raging waters and carried to the gravel shallows where they were gradually buried by silt and floating debris.

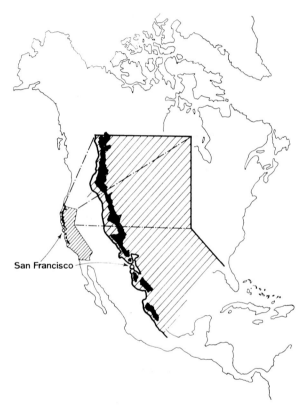

The redwood territory.

The redwood is a unique species of tree that grows nowhere in the world outside a narrow, thirty-mile-wide belt that stretches along the Pacific Coast for some 500 miles, from just north of Monterey, California, to the southwestern corner of Oregon. This, plus the fact that redwoods are among the most majestic trees on earth, makes it our national duty to see that they are properly protected. Redwoods are

not in imminent danger of extinction at the hands of the lumber industry, but (1) too many of the largest ones are being cut and too many acres of virgin red-wood forest are privately owned and managed for timber production, and (2) the existing redwood parks are still not "safe" because they are not ecological entities. These parks are still too small; they are limited to river bottom stands where the most spec-tacular trees are found and do not include the higher areas, the watersheds of their streams and rivers, the places where floods originate. These higher areas, where trees are smaller, are still being logged and therefore are sites of potentially catastrophic erosion. Unless they too are brought under control, the ex-isting redwood parks can never really be "safe." Fortunately, this problem is well recognized, and the Save-the-Redwoods League (discussed more fully in Chapter XVI) is making every effort to include these vitally important tracts within the boundaries of already existing parks. By July 1966, working in cooperation with the State of California, the League had already acquired around 75 per cent of the Upper Basin area of Bull Creek. It had initiated positive bank protection within the park on critical bends, made sure that gravel could move freely along the river channel, and instigated a system of fire protection within the upper reaches of the watershed to promote the growth of protective vegetation. All these ambitious and vitally important programs are carried out entirely on a voluntary basis.

The coast redwood *(Sequoia sempervirens)* is different from, although closely related to, the "big tree," the "giant" sequoia *(Sequoia gigantea)* which occurs far-ther inland to the south (see picture pages 97–100) and is a cousin of the bald cypress of the southeast *(Taxodium distichum,* see picture page 58). Redwoods grow considerably taller than giant sequoias, but their trunks never reach the awe-inspiring dimensions of those trees, their maximum diameter seldom ex-ceeding twenty feet. The tallest redwoods, which are not necessarily the oldest, are always found in fertile river bottom lands. At higher elevations, where climatic conditions are more severe and water usually less abundant, trees grow just as old but never as big. The age of the largest redwoods is probably less than 2,500 years; the oldest sequoias are possibly thirty-five centuries old.

70

Redwoods are among the fastest-growing trees. It is not uncommon for a vigorous young tree to increase its diameter at a rate of an inch or more a year, and at least one redwood that grew under favorable conditions is known to have reached a trunk diameter of over six feet measured at chest height within only 150 years. (This specimen sprouted from the root system of a parent stump after the Russians logged the area to build Fort Ross in 1812–1815; it stands on privately owned timberland in California's Sonoma County.) Other scientifically measured redwoods growing on average, good, and excellent sites, have reached diameters of 25.3, 28.4, and 31.0 inches, respectively, within a hundred years. This rapid rate of growth makes redwoods eminently suitable as a commercial cash crop on a continuous-yield basis and should assure the perpetual existence of our redwood forests.

An interesting fact about redwoods is that these tallest of all trees have some of the smallest of all cones; of a handful of redwood cones gathered around the "Founders' Tree" and now lying on my desk the average length is slightly less than one inch. (Some cones of the much smaller sugar pine which I collected in the High Sierra measure up to eighteen inches in length, and the literature mentions cones up to twenty-four inches long.) The root system of redwoods is also very shallow in comparison to their size, seldom penetrating more than ten feet into the ground, although individual roots may radiate 100 feet from the trunk. This shallowness makes these trees easily undercut and toppled by floods. It also explains why famous large trees in public parks are usually fenced in: to prevent the ground above the roots from being compacted by hordes of visitors' feet and thus made almost impervious to rain.

When a redwood is cut its root usually does not die, but immediately starts growing several new sprouts from the edges of the cut: within a few years a "fairy ring" pattern is formed around the stump. Competition for water and sun, however, rapidly reduces this number, and within twenty-five years there may be a maximum of only ten to fifteen trees remaining in the circle. Most of these will survive for some fifty years before continuing competition further reduces their number. Tree farmers have found it unwise to thin these sprouts too early because an early reduction to five or six trees well spaced around the perimeter of the stump only encourages the growth of more sprouts.

A redwood forest that has been clean-logged will in time re-establish itself, provided the life-giving soil has not eroded away. Where slash and logging debris have been removed by burning, fireweed is the first to move into the area and soon will form a temporary solid field. In river bottom land, light-loving trees such as willow, alder, laurel, and an occasional big-leaf maple will appear next, together with various shrubs and weeds. On the slopes madroña (see picture page 60), tanbark oak, and black oak, along with several species of shrubs, may dominate during the first few years.

However, during the first years after harvesting, redwood sprouts will quickly shoot up from stump roots left on the clean-cut site. The seedlings of other conifers such as Douglas fir and spruce will follow, delayed by the partial shade of the brush and hardwoods. But these shade-tolerating conifers (many of which actually require shade during the pre-reproductive years) will doggedly persist for several decades until they finally break through the crowns of the hardwoods and eventually take over the site as associates of the redwoods.

Alders may persist among the redwoods and other conifers as long as seventy-five years, and laurel even longer. But within fewer than fifty years, the new stand of timber may be well over 80 per cent conifer, with redwood dominating. Redwoods of seedling origin and Douglas fir will eventually catch up with the stump-origin redwoods, since the explosive initial height growth of the stump sprouts tapers off after the first few years. Finally, a stage of plant succession will be reached when the redwoods crowd out all other species of trees and completely dominate the site. This final state, about which more is said in Chapter XII, is called the "climax forest."

Picture pages

76—80. Redwoods in Humboldt Redwoods State Park in northern California.

IX
Leaves

Leaves are among the most important structures in nature. They are factories which make plant food from water and air—it is plants that sustain all animal life, including the life of man. The process by which this miracle is performed is *photosynthesis*. The power which makes it possible is light. In highly simplified form—because actually many steps are involved, some of them still not fully understood—the reaction that takes place during photosynthesis is

$$6CO_2 + 6H_2O + 674 \text{ kcal.} \longrightarrow C_6H_{12}O_6 + 6O_2.$$

carbon   water   energy   sugar   oxygen
dioxide

This is truly the formula of life, perhaps the most important equation in the world. In ordinary language it means that, under the influence of light, six molecules of carbon dioxide combine with six of water to produce one molecule of sugar and six of oxygen. This single molecule of sugar, multiplied by the astronomical number of such molecules synthesized at any given time, is the basis of life.

It is impossible to grasp the true extent of photosynthesis in quantitative terms, although it is possible to express it in the form of figures. Who can visualize a thousand million tons? Nevertheless, it is in such terms that we must think when we try to grasp the magnitude of photosynthesis, which, in translation, means "putting together with light." This is what scientists have found:

Each year the plants of the world transform some 60,000 million tons of atmospheric carbon into an estimated 150,000 million tons of sugar. (Man's annual sugar harvest amounts to a trifling 39 million tons.) Sugar is energy in chemically fixed form, and if the latent energy of the entire plant-produced mass of sugar were released (by burning, for example), the liberated power would come to approximately two quintillion kilocalories. This amount is about 100 times greater than the amount of energy we could produce if we were to burn all the coal mined in the entire world during one year.

Without photosynthesis we would have no wheat, rice, corn, or potatoes; no flowers and no trees; no leaves and no grass. As a matter of fact, there would be no plants. Without plants there would be no plant-eating animals—no cows or horses, sheep or goats, chicken or ducks, antelopes or elephants. And without plant-eating animals there would be no flesh-eating animals—no lions or wolves, no cats or dogs, no eagles or owls and, of course, no man. Without photosynthesis there would be no organic compounds or products of any kind whatsoever, and, except for a few kinds of autotrophic bacteria, the earth would be as lifeless as the moon. The action of leaves makes our planet suitable for life.

It is hard to believe that anything so important should take place within objects as small and ordinary as leaves. But unimpressive size is offset by astronomical numbers, and what appears simple because it is small is actually a chemical factory of marvelous complexity.

A leaf consists of three main parts: epidermis, mesophyll, and vascular bundles.

The *epidermis* is a continuous "skin" that covers both sides of a leaf. It is formed by a single layer of transparent, interlocking cells, which are covered by the *cuticle*, a waxy film designed to protect the leaf's internal tissues from excessive dehydration. Numerous openings called *stomates* (or *stomata*), which in trees are located only on the undersides of leaves, perforate the epidermis and permit a two-way exchange between the atmosphere and the inside of the leaf of such gases as carbon dioxide, water vapor, and oxygen. The stomates are protected by two curved, sausage-like epidermal cells called *guard cells* which, through changes in their internal hydraulic pressure, open or close the stomates in accordance with atmospheric conditions and the needs of the leaf.

The *mesophyll* contains the food-producing machinery of the leaf, specifically, the *chloroplasts*. These are the specialized bodies imbedded within the cytoplasm of the mesophyll cells which contain *chlorophyll*, the green pigment which is the basis of photosynthesis. The chloroplasts are unbelievably small and their number unimaginably large—it has been estimated that each square millimeter (each 1/625 square inch) of an average leaf contains some 400,000 chloroplasts. No wonder that the total area exposed to light of all the chloroplasts within the leaves of a large deciduous tree may add up to some 140 square miles!

The *vascular bundles*—the veins—are composed of specialized strands of tissue which simultaneously provide support for the leaf and act as conductors of liquids. They are located about halfway between the upper and lower surfaces of the leaf and consist of two kinds of tissue: thick-walled, woody *xylem* cells, which conduct water and, like the ribs of an umbrella, provide mechanical support, and thin-walled *phloem* cells which serve as pipelines for liquid foods. Together they form a conducting system which, branching from one or several main veins, permeates the entire leaf to such an extent that no cell of the mesophyll is more than a few cell lengths away from vascular tissue.

Man has so far been unable to duplicate the process of photosynthesis in the laboratory. This much is known: The crucial transformation of radiant energy (provided by light) into chemical energy (stored in the form of glucose or plant sugar) occurs in the chloroplasts. Each chloroplast consists of hundreds of microscopically small, coin-shaped bodies called *grana* which in turn contain the bead-shaped *quantasomes*, the individual photosynthetic units tightly packed with light-sensitive chlorophyll molecules. Sunlight striking the leaf interacts with these molecules, which absorb part of the radiation and thereby get excited to a higher energy level. These light-activated chlorophyll molecules now combine with molecules of water (brought to the leaves from the roots), splitting them in the process. The oxygen atoms from the shattered water molecules escape into the air, while the by now highly activated hydrogen atoms stay behind in the chloroplasts. In a series of complex but virtually instantaneous reactions these energy-laden hydrogen atoms combine with low-energy carbon compounds derived from carbon dioxide previously taken by the leaf from the air to produce molecules of a highly reactive compound called *phosphoglyceric acid* (PGA). Finally, molecules of PGA combine to form the energy-rich end product, the carbohydrate compound sugar.

The sugar produced by plants is *glucose* (also called grape sugar, or dextrose), the only naturally occurring form of sugar. Glucose consists of carbon dioxide and water, but, since solar radiation was absorbed in its synthesis, the energy content of this compound is higher than the sum of that of its constituents. This extra energy powers the life processes of all plants and, for that matter, the life processes of all animals. So, ultimately, the entire machinery of life runs on fuel provided by a star, and all living things are part cosmic radiation.

The glucose produced in the chloroplasts provides a plant with both food and raw material. Food is "fuel," i.e., energy in chemically fixed form which, when released, powers all the life processes of plants, the most obvious one being growth; raw material is needed for the construction of the new tissues added constantly by the growing plant. Among the substances into which glucose is converted are cellulose, a building material; starch, a form of carbohydrate particularly suited to storage; fats and oils, which provide energy when reconverted into sugar with the aid of enzymes; and proteins, complex compounds known as *amino acids*, consisting of glucose in various combinations with nitrogen, sulphur, and occasionally phosphorus. These are essential to the maintenance of all life, but many amino acids indispensable to animal nutrition, and almost as many vitally important to man, are synthethized only by plants. And so it is again on plants that man and animal depend, not only for their structurally essential carbon and energy-furnishing carbohydrates, but also for some of the subtler ingredients indispensable to health and growth.

In the process of manufacturing glucose, leaves give off large quantities of oxygen. This liberated oxygen is just as important for the continuing existence of life as the sugar which plants produce. For, although oxygen is one of the most abundant elements on earth, most of it is chemically fixed in the form of water or as an oxide—a combination of oxygen with another element such as aluminium, calcium, iron, magnesium, silicon, sodium. Large amounts of oxygen are constantly withdrawn from the air by the respiration of living things, by the burning of coal, oil, wood, garbage, and other organic substances, and by natural oxidation processes such as the weathering of rocks. In the course of time, were it not for the activities of plants, these factors would combine to extract all oxygen from the atmosphere. For although plants use up oxygen in respiration, the amount is smaller than that released by the disassociation of water in photosynthesis. In the end, more oxygen is released into the atmosphere than is withdrawn from it. As a matter of fact, most scientists now believe that originally the atmosphere contained less oxygen than it contains today and that its present high content of almost 21 per cent by volume is largely due to the activity of plants. If this process were ever to be reversed—if plants should use more oxygen than they free—life as we know it would become extinct.

Leaves are not only among the biologically most important, but also the aesthetically most beautiful

dius of less than a mile from my house, I collected a basketful of fallen leaves belonging to the white oak group, looking particularly for differences of form. Of these I photographed fifteen especially interesting specimens. I enlarged the negative and placed the print on a light-table, covered it with a sheet of translucent paper, and carefully traced the outline of each leaf.

The accompanying sketch gives an idea of the many ways in which a basic design can be varied: the char-

structures in nature. Their wealth of form is infinite, and, although normally all the leaves of the same species adhere to the same design, no two leaves are ever exactly alike. This adherence to design makes leaves a valuable aid in identifying trees, while diversification of detail within the frame of a specific pattern makes leaves fascinating subjects for comparative studies and sheer aesthetic enjoyment. Just before the snow blanketed the ground, within a ra-

acter of all the leaves is more or less the same, since all are based on the same *pinnately lobed* pattern which makes them instantly recognizable as belonging to the white oak group. But the details of execution vary widely. That such variations of a theme are not an isolated phenomenon, but actually quite common, is demonstrated by the following tracing of the photographs of the leaves of eight different species of trees characterized by a *palmately lobed* design.

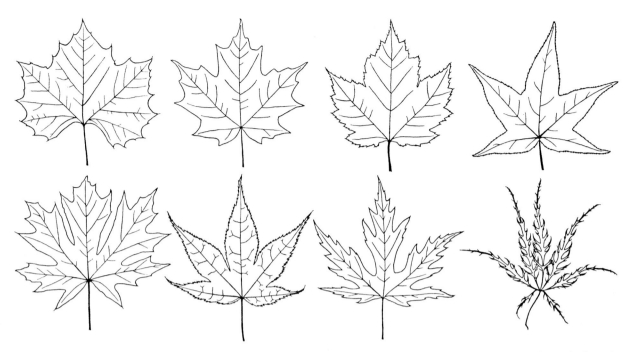

Top: Sycamore, sugar maple, red maple, sweet gum. Bottom: big leaf maple, Japanese maple, silver maple, cutleaf maple.

For purposes of identification, leaves can be classified according to several characteristics as follows:

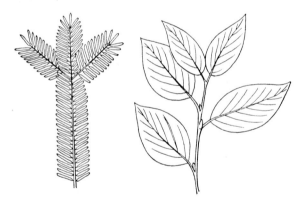

Trees with needle-like or scale-like leaves vs. broad-leaved trees. This easily made distinction instantly eliminates a large number of trees from consideration. If the tree has small needle-like or tiny scale-like leaves it belongs to the order of *Conifers*—the "softwoods," or "evergreens" (although the larches lose their needles in winter): pine, fir, spruce, hemlock, cedar, cypress, larch, sequoia, yew. On the other hand, if the tree has broad leaves (i.e., leaves that are thin and flat, membranous, easily wilting) it belongs to the *deciduous trees*—those which annually shed their leaves in fall, such as maple, oak, birch—or to the southern broad-leaved evergreens such as live oak, magnolia, fig (exception: ginkgo, a *Gymnosperm* like our conifers), whose leaves are usually more leathery and tough.

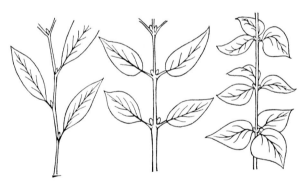

Leaf arrangement on the twig. The most common arrangement is *spiral*, one at a node (alternately), attached to the twig. Only a relatively small number of trees grow their leaves *paired*, i.e., attached opposite to each other on the twig; since there are only a few their names can easily be remembered by the mnemonic "mad horse" in which the letter "m" stands for maple, "a" for ash, "d" for dogwood, and "horse" for horse–chestnut (and also for buckeye with its horse–chestnut–like leaves). Very few trees and shrubs have leaves that *grow in threes* (whorled) such as, for example, the catalpas (see drawing at right in the sketch above).

Simple or compound leaves. A *simple leaf* consists of only a single leaf blade and a stalk by which it is attached to the woody twig. A *compound leaf* consists of three

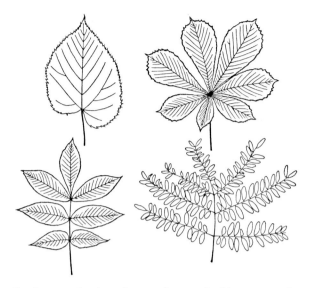

Leaf types: simple, palmate, pinnate, doubly compound.

(rarely two) to several dozen leaflets, each attached by its stalk to a *midrib* which is not woody but similar to the stalks of the individual leaflets. To determine whether a leaf is simple or compound, examine the angle formed by the leaf stalk and the twig: if it contains a tiny *axillary bud*, the leaf is simple; if no such bud exists, the structure is a leaflet—a component of a compound leaf—and the axillary bud will be found in the angle formed by the compound leaf's midrib and the twig. If there is no axillary bud in this angle, the leaf is doubly compound, and the elusive axillary bud will be located in the angle between the main rib and the twig.

Types of compound leaves. If all the leaflets of a compound leaf radiate from a single point, the leaf is *palmate*, or *palmately compound* (it resembles the underside of a hand with its fingers spread); a typical example is the horse-chestnut leaf. If the leaflets are arranged on both sides of a midrib or central stem, the leaf is *pinnate*, or *pinnately compound* (it resembles a feather, the leaflets corresponding to the barbs and the midrib to the quill); typical examples are the leaves of black locust, ash, and hickory. If the midrib is branched (a relatively rare type), the leaf is *twice pinnately compound*, or *doubly compound;* typical examples are the leaves of the honey locust, Hercules'-club, and Kentucky coffee tree.

Leaf margins occur in almost as many different forms as leaf shapes, but, in contrast, are very constant as far as specific species are concerned and provide valuable

Leaf margins: red oak, white oak, chestnut oak, mulberry, slippery elm, and catalpa.

aids in identifying trees. Some of the patterns which leaf margins can assume are illustrated above in the form of photograph tracings.

Leaves of radically different forms are found on only very few trees, for example mulberry and sassafras (see picture pages 82 and 86). Both trees produce leaves that can have one of three forms: unlobed, mitten-shaped (two-lobed), and three-lobed; all three forms are usually found on the same tree. Yet the two trees are easily distinguished since the margins of mulberry leaves are toothed and those of the sassafras leaves are smooth (above, top: sassafras; bottom: mulberry).

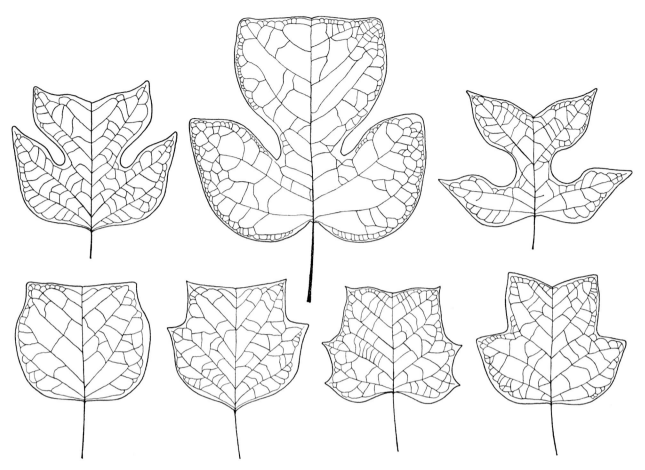

Leaf shapes vary considerably within each species. Because this is essentially true of all tree species, I personally attach little value to the leaf-shape diagrams of tree-identification books which distinguish between circular, oval, elliptical, ovate, lance, triangular, diamond, fan, and heart shapes. The leaves of the flowering dogwood, for example, vary from a rather narrow and elongated to an almost circular shape, and those of the tulip tree show an even greater diversity of form. I have collected a comparative series of leaves from tulip trees and, because I find them not only instructive but also very beautiful, show here sketches traced over actual photographs to illustrate the great variety of shapes and sizes that can occur among the leaves of the same tree species (see line drawing above).

Particularly typical leaf shapes. Some tree-identification books give the impression that all one needs to identify a tree is a sample of its leaves. This may or may not be true, depending on the particular species, but it certainly is not the rule. Many trees have leaves that are so similar to those of other kinds that even experts find it difficult, if not impossible, to make an unqualified identification solely on the basis of a leaf. Oak leaves, for example, can easily be identified as belonging to the white oaks, the black oaks, or the live oaks; but to say authoritatively to which species within the group a leaf belongs is often impossible. In such a case, the respective tree can be identified only by other means—in this case, by the shape of the acorn and its cup. Similarly, the leaves of many willows are virtually indistinguishable from one another, and the leaves of certain other trees, such as sweet birch and hop hornbeam, are extraordinarily similar. In this instance identification is best based on characteristics of flowers, seeds, and bark.

On the other hand, there are a number of trees with more or less unique leaves. Prominent among these are mulberry and sassafras, whose leaves have been shown in drawings and can be seen in photographs on picture pages 82 and 86; sweet gum (picture page 83), whose star-shaped leaves have one of the most appeal-

Top row: sweet gum, slippery elm, dogwood. Bottom row: ginkgo, largetoothed aspen.

ing of all leaf patterns; tulip trees with unique notched tips *(emarginate,* see previous drawings and photographs on picture pages 88–89); slippery elm, whose leaves can be recognized instantly by the extremely rough, sandpaper-like texture of the upper side of the leaf; flowering dogwood with its smooth, centrally slightly creased, oppositely arranged leaves with their characteristically curved secondary veins; large-toothed aspen with hard, roundish leaves studded peripherally with coarse blunt teeth; and that "living fossil," the ginkgo, with leathery, fan-shaped, often split and somewhat tattered leaves (see picture page 30). The tracings (above) of photographs of actual leaves will help to identify these trees while at the same time testifying to the seemingly endless diversity of their leaves.

Picture pages 81–96

81. Young Danish beech in spring foliage. Tens of thousands of brand-new leaves unfurl their perfect little shapes, forming a canopy of sheerest translucent green.

82. White mulberry *(Morus alba).* This tree, whose many-shaped, lobed and toothed leaves are the food of the silkworm, is an Asian import introduced to America in an attempt to establish a silk industry.

83. Sweet gum *(Liquidambar styraciflua).* The five-pointed, star-shaped leaves offer instant identification. Sweet gum is a relatively large tree whose one-inch spherical dangling fruit is similar to that of sycamore

except that it is hard and covered with claw-like prickles—another way to recognize this tree.

84. Sycamore (*Platanus occidentalis;* see also picture pages 7 and 45). The leaves somewhat resemble those of maple, but are generally larger, coarser, and more shallow-lobed. An unmistakable clue is the swollen base of the leaf stalk which does not end flat as in other leaves but hollow, with a cone-shaped indentation which fits snugly over the winter bud.

85. Sugar maple (*Acer saccharum;* see also picture pages 18–19). The maples are the only North American trees with opposite palmately lobed leaves, and therefore easy to recognize as a group. Of the several species, the two most common in the Northeast are sugar maple and red maple. To tell them apart, note that sugar maple leaves are five to eight inches long, generally five-lobed with moderately deep, more or less rounded, U-shaped notches between lobes; the underside is usually pale green. Red maple leaves are smaller, two to five inches long, three- to five-lobed with moderately deep, sharp-angled, V-shaped notches between lobes; the underside is usually whitened and the edges less smooth, with smaller, more numerous teeth.

86. Sassafras (*Sassafras albidum*). Like mulberry, this tree produces leaves in three different shapes: a smooth, elliptical type; a two-lobed "mitten-shaped" type; and a three-lobed type, all of which are on the same tree. But whereas the edges of mulberry leaves have coarse teeth, those of the sassafras are smooth.

87. Ailanthus, or tree of heaven (*Ailanthus altissima*). This is the backyard tree which thrives where nothing else will grow, a "weed-tree," which sprouts amidst the rubbish or from cracks between pavement and wall. It is also one of the fastest-growing trees—increases of eight feet per year are not unusual.

88–89. Tulip tree, or yellow poplar (*Liriodendron tulipifera*). At the left is a seedling tree in its second year; at the right, a typical leaf of a mature tree. Leaf shape, however, is subject to considerable variation as shown in the preceding drawings. But the invariable clue is the notched leaf tip.

90. Hercules'-club, or Devil's walking stick (*Aralia*

spinosa). Its enormous double-compound leaves are larger than those of any other North American tree, almost four feet in length and over two feet in width. In addition to the colossal leaves, this strange and usually small tree has vicious prickles which generously cover trunk, branches, and leaf stalks.

91. Slippery elm (*Ulmus rubra*). What at first glance may appear to be a pinnately compound leaf is actually a shoot carrying alternate simple leaves. To distinguish between slippery elm and American elm, feel the surfaces of the leaves. Both are sandpaper rough, but American elm feels rough only if rubbed in one direction; a slippery elm leaf, which is also coarser-textured, feels rough no matter which way you rub it.

92. Coconut palm (*Cocos nucifera*). Marvel at the structure of this leaf, the precision with which its parts are joined, the evenness of spacing, the graceful tapering of the stem. The ridges on the palm trunk at the left are leaf scars.

93. Washingtonia palm (*Washingtonia robusta*). What at first might look like a thatched hut belonging to one of the more primitive African tribes is actually a living palm whose trunk is covered with masses of dead unshed leaves. This is typical of Washingtonia, a fan-leaf palm native to Baja California and Mexico, but widely planted in Florida, the Gulf states, and California. Few people have seen these palms with their "grass-skirts" on, owing to the care taken by the park departments of cities, who trim the dead leaves as soon as possible to prevent vandals from setting fire to the trees, a "sport" which, of course, kills them.

94. Pandanus (*Pandanus* sp.). Like a many-eyed monster, this tree-like plant seems to glower from the swampy banks of a jungle stream. But what looks like eyes are only leaf scars.

95. Traveler's-tree (*Ravenala madagascariensis*). The photograph shows the basis of the enormous leaves which grow up to twenty feet long and resemble those of a banana tree.

96. Palm leaf stalks. The vicious-looking teeth that cover the edges of the leaf stalks of this unidentified palm prevent animals from stealing its fruit.

80

X
The Biggest Living Things

Not for nothing is "big tree" one of the popular names of the giant sequoia *(Sequoia gigantea)*—mature sequoias are by far the most massive living organisms on earth. The largest and most massive animal that ever lived (including the giant dinosaurs) is the blue whale *(Sibbaldus musculus)*; the largest recorded specimen measured 108 feet in length and weighed 152.8 tons. Compare this with the dimensions of the two largest sequoias, the "General Sherman" and "General Grant," the star attractions of California's Sequoia National Park:

Dimensions	Sherman	Grant
Height above mean base	272.4 feet	267.4 feet
Circumference at base	101.6 feet	107.6 feet
Maximum diameter at base	36.5 feet	40.3 feet
Mean diameter at base	32.2 feet	33.3 feet
Diameter 60 feet above ground	17.5 feet	18.8 feet
Diameter 120 feet above ground	17.0 feet	15.0 feet
Diameter 180 feet above ground	14.0 feet	12.9 feet
Height to first large branch	130.0 feet	129.0 feet
Diameter of largest branch	6.8 feet	4.5 feet
Weight of trunk (estimate)	625.0 tons	565.0 tons
Total volume of trunk	50,010 cu. ft.	45,232 cu. ft.

The total weight of the General Sherman Tree is estimated at more than 1,000 tons. This single tree contains enough lumber to build forty five-room houses. Thirty railroad cars would be needed to haul the trunk, which would have to be cut up into sections since its basal diameter alone averages more than thirty-two feet.

Still taller than these two giants is the McKinley Tree, which stands 291 feet and is the tallest known sequoia. This tree stands all by itself just off Congress Trail, the spectacular loop walk in Sequoia National Park. However, because it is slimmer and less massive that the other two trees, it does not give the same impression of unbelievable hugeness.

Of all the wonders of the world—man-made as well as natural, including the Taj Mahal and the Golden Gate Bridge, the Grand Canyon and Niagara Falls—the most overwhelming is, in my opinion, the "House Group" of giant sequoias in Sequoia National Park (picture pages 98–99). No photograph or description can convey the impact which this congregation of giants makes. As a rule sequoias occur singly and widely spaced, intermixed with a multitude of lesser trees. Their incredible dimensions and spectacular fox-red to weathered-bronze and gray-purple colors, which seem to shift with every change of light, make them seem like relics from some antediluvian "lost world." Seen individually, and particularly at a distance, single sequoias sometimes lack the emphasizing element of scale—a sequoia seen from a distance of 500 feet can be mistaken for an ordinary tree only fifty feet away, with the surrounding sugar pines and their five-foot-in-diameter trunks shrunk to the dimensions of more familiar trees. But when several of these monsters stand together in a group and we walk up to them and touch their satin-soft cinnamon bark, the result is impressive.

I spent an entire week in this magic forest in an attempt to capture the uncapturable on film. Again and again I went back to carefully selected groups of trees, studying them from all sides and angles, observing them in every conceivable light, thoroughly familiarizing myself with their personalities. I had seen sequoias before, I had analyzed dozens of the best photographs of these trees, and I knew that I would be up against an almost insoluble photographic problem: how to infuse my pictures with a sense of scale. I was determined not to include that most familiar of all units of scale, the human figure, which, in contrast to its own relative smallness, would make the trees in the photographs appear huge. Instead of doing the obvious and shooting my pictures with a wide-angle lens, I stepped back as far as circumstances permitted and used telephoto lenses in an effort to preserve the natural proportions of these trees. I wasted a great amount of color film before I finally admitted defeat and realized that if I ever expected to show sequoias in their proper scale I would have to include a human figure. And so, in the end, I asked Wysse to rest near one of the giants—a female Gulliver among Brobdingnagian trees.

Sequoias are the last survivors of a race of trees whose lineage goes back some 75 million years to the Tertiary Age. A relative of theirs, the "dawn redwood" *Metasequoia*, made botanical history in 1946 when it was discovered in a remote area of central China. This tree, a close relative of our present redwoods and sequoias, is a veritable "living fossil" insofar as it is virtually identical with extinct trees that grew millions of years ago. Once a common forest tree, *Metasequoia* disappeared from the North American continent by the end of the Miocene and became confined to Asia, where it

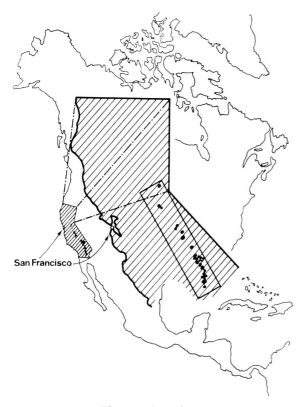

The sequoia territory.

succeeded in surviving in a single location so remote from civilization that it previously had escaped scientific notice. Similarly, the giant sequoias, once common forest trees whose range included large areas of Europe and North America, Siberia, China, Alaska, Japan, and even parts of the Southern Hemisphere, had in the course of time reduced their territory until, today, they occur in only a single spot on earth: the western slopes of the Sierra Nevada in California at elevations from 3,000 to 8,900 feet. Today sequoias are no longer found in pure stands, but only in association with other trees, primarily sugar pine, ponderosa pine, white fir, incense cedar, and California black oak. Their total territory is extremely small and encompasses only 35,000 acres. They occur northward as far as the Middle Fork of the American River where, thirty-

five miles south of Soda Springs, a group of six comparatively small trees has been found. Their southern limit is the border of California's Tulare and Kern counties. Their main range is the Kaweah and Tule watersheds where sequoia forests cover several thousand acres.

Not too long ago sequoias were ruthlessly cut down by lumbermen, although they are not suited to lumbering because of their unwieldy size and because their immense trunks tend to shatter like glass on impact with the ground, wasting large quantities of wood and making the rest less useful commercially. To me, cutting a giant sequoia for profit is a crime, and the Big Stump Basin near the Grant Grove entrance to Sequoia National Park seems to me an eloquent monument to man's most vicious and despicable instincts. Fortunately, farsighted men under the inspired leadership of John Muir and Colonel George W. Stewart realized the uniqueness of these majestic trees before it was too late and, after prolonged struggles with vested interests, were able to persuade Congress in 1890 to remove the largest part of the sequoia forest from commercial exploitation and set it aside as a National Park. Today, approximately 98 per cent of all the remaining giant sequoias are preserved in some seventy state and federal groves and parks.

Unlike the coast redwoods which, when cut, send up new shoots from the cambium layer of the stump and thereby are able to renew themselves, sequoias can reproduce themselves only from seeds. These seeds—gossamer golden membranes one-eighth to one-quarter of an inch in length—enclose a seed the size of a needle tip and are so light that several thousand would be required to balance the weight of an acorn. Four to six of these seeds lie under each scale of a two- to three-and-one-half-inch cone, which is firm and hard and resembles a small fragmentation hand grenade.

The bark of sequoias is unlike that of any other tree in both texture and color: a beautiful cinnamon brown with overtones of rust, purple, and ash-gray, often flecked with black, the reminder of fires that swept through the forest ages ago. Shiny highlights enliven its satiny texture, which is warm and resilient to the touch. The bark is some two feet thick, strongly impregnated with tannin, and highly resistant to insect pests and fire. A few years ago a large sequoia was struck by lightning and ignited; although this occurred in July, the fire smoldered quietly without flaring up or seriously injuring the tree until it was put out by a snowstorm in October.

The root system is very shallow, forming an enormous mat that may cover several acres. This shallowness presents the greatest danger to the life of old sequoias, because it affords little anchorage for the top-heavy trees, which occasionally topple without apparent cause. A tree growing at the edge of a meadow is particularly subject to this danger because the side facing the meadow may gradually settle in the damper soil. The tree begins to lean and, when the roots can no longer hold the off-center weight, crashes into the meadow. The fallen giant may then obstruct the free flow of spring and surface water, which in turn may cause over-saturation of the ground at the base of nearby trees, which eventually may share its fate. One such fallen giant lies on Circle Meadow just off the Congress Trail in Sequoia National Park, and there is no better way to realize the immensity of these trees than to walk the full length of its fallen trunk. Another giant sequoia, which toppled on August 22, 1953, lies near the Founders' Group at the farthest corner of the Congress Trail loop. The dimensions of its shattered trunk stagger the imagination. No one who has climbed this monstrous bole will ever doubt that the giant sequoias are truly the largest living things on earth.

Picture pages 97–100

97. Trunks of a twin sequoia rise near the General Grant Tree parking area in Sequoia National Park. This picture was taken early one morning in June, with the sun backlighting the tree and outlining the two trunks with finely etched seams of light. The lovely blue in the background is the effect of haze—atmospheric moisture that has not yet been dissipated by the still cool air. Lack of scale—absence of such familiar objects as people or cars–makes it impossible to appreciate the enormous size of these trunks, each with a diameter of about twelve feet.

98–99. A view of the "House Group" of giant sequoias in Sequoia National Park. Strolling quietly among these giants, listening to the air moving through sky-high branches with a hum as old as the drone of distant waves, smelling the fragrance of evergreen boughs, of nearby incense cedar and sugar pine, is an unforgettable experience. Not far from here, with its back against a white fir, is a simple bench, offering a superlative view of these majestic trees.

100. A group of thousand-year-old sequoias in Sequoia National Park. The contrast between the reddish boles and the evergreen branches is a sheer aesthetic delight. Backlight weaves halos of light wherever the sun can penetrate the canopy formed by the crowns of these gigantic trees.

XI
Roots, Thorns, and Spines

Every tree has a root or a system of roots. The function of the root is to absorb water and minerals in solution from the soil; to transport these to the aerial portions of the tree; to serve as a reservoir for food; and to anchor the tree to the ground.

Everyone has seen the exposed roots of wind-felled trees, a twisted mass of brown woody snakes that vary in size from massive to pencil thin. These "visible" components of a root, however, consist mainly of rigid, nonconducting wood. The parts that perform the vitally important task of supplying the tree with water and minerals—the *root tips* and *root hairs*—are all but invisible.

When a seed germinates, the single root, which grows downward, soon gives rise to lateral branches, which grow and produce other branches, which in turn branch out again. Each branch terminates in a *root tip* with a minute protective, thimble-like *root cap* at its very end. This is the active part of the root. It is only within this zone, less than an inch long and thin as a thread, that the root grows in length. As it grows, pushing its protective cap ahead of it, it twists and snakes, probing the soil for water and nutrients, which it absorbs through a multitude of single-celled, almost microscopically fine *root hairs*. These root hairs, which cover only the growing tip of the root, are short-lived and are constantly replaced; they literally number in the billions. Although no one has ever counted all the hairs in the root system of a large tree, quantitative studies of the roots of rye, a grass-like plant, have produced the following almost unbelievable results: after only four months of growth, a single plant had developed a total of 378 miles of roots consisting of some 14 million separate branches with more than 14 billion root hairs. The average speed of root growth was found to be three miles per day. The total surface of the root hairs alone was calculated to be in excess of 4,000 square feet, equal to the floor area of three or four one-family houses. In conjunction with the surface

area of the root proper, this totaled more than 6,500 square feet of root surface, which, however—and this is what really strains credulity—was contained within a volume of soil that measured only about two cubic feet. This prodigious growth enables roots to absorb large quantities of water from soil that appears virtually dry. It becomes clear that this ability is a vital necessity for the survival of a tree when one learns that a single birch may require as much as 900 gallons of water per day. Molecule by molecule this water has to be absorbed by the probing root hairs and passed along from cell to cell throughout the length of the root and through the trunk and branches until it reaches the leaves, where it is used in photosynthesis and finally evaporated into the air.

Roots take up nutrients from the soil in mineral solution without any serious flow back. Still more remarkable, roots can absorb inorganic material in solution *against* a concentration gradient, i.e., they take up ions even though ion concentration is higher within the root than in the soil solution. The absorbing cells must furthermore be selective, able to distinguish between nutrients needed by the tree and useless or harmful substances. This delicate task is accomplished with the aid of selectively permeable membranes which permit free passage to certain kinds of ions but make penetration difficult or impossible for others. So what at a glance may seem merely a mass of dirty roots is actually an absorbing and conducting organ of incredible complexity and sensitivity.

In addition to acting as a water pump, a gatherer of nutrients, and an analytical laboratory, roots provide anchorage for the tree. This may seem elemental, but it is actually quite an accomplishment if one considers that, for example, redwood trees 300 feet tall and very top-heavy have been held up securely for 2,000 years by a root system that penetrates only ten to fifteen feet into the ground. This feat is possible because of literally millions of individual roots and rootlets digging into the ground, which press against individual pebbles and stones, and wedge and compact the soil to such an extent that the entire mass of gravel, rocks, and sand encompassed by the entire root system becomes one immense and virtually homogenous platform which supports and counterbalances the aerial portion of the tree.

85

◀ 98—100

Three basic types of root systems can be distinguished, although it must be understood that the first two are far from being mutually exclusive. All root systems begin as tap roots, and the course of root development is determined partly by genetics and partly by the character of the soil environment. Furthermore, few trees have truly fibrous root systems in the sense that grasses do (a multitude of hair-like roots incapable of secondary thickening); this kind is probably most closely approached by the roots of creek-side willows. Finally, adventitious roots are secondary structures developed by trees which started out with normal radicular roots.

The *fibrous root system* (above) has a very large number of more or less horizontally growing roots that lie relatively close to the surface and branch out again and again into increasingly finer strands until the entire soil is pervaded by a thick mat of root fibers. Trees with this type of shallow root system are elm, birch, beech, spruce, hemlock, fir, redwood, and sequoia. Contrary to widespread belief, this lateral spread, as well as that of the tap root system described below, usually extends far beyond the spread of the tree's crown. Accordingly, watering a tree near its trunk accom-

plishes very little because the largest number of water-absorbing root tips are found near the periphery of the root system.

The *tap root system* (below) is characterized by a main root that, like a massive pole, penetrates deeply into the ground and is supplemented by a loose network of secondary, smaller lateral roots. This kind of root provides a more effective anchorage for a tree than a fibrous root system, a fact much in evidence after every hurricane: whereas elms, hemlocks, spruce, and many other trees with shallow fibrous root systems are toppled everywhere the tap root trees—oak, walnut, hickory, pine—are usually left standing. As a rule, trees that have tap roots are more difficult to transplant than trees with a fibrous root system.

Adventitious roots are roots produced in an abnormal position, such as the aerial roots of banyan trees (see picture pages 108–109). This kind of auxiliary root issues either from the side of the trunk or from a branch, often at a great height, and grows downward until it penetrates the soil. These roots give the tree additional support while also making it possible for branches to extend horizontally to normally unattainable distances; aerial roots dropped to the ground at certain intervals support the limb like pillars supporting a bridge (picture pages 104–105). Of special interest are the adventitious roots of the mangrove (picture pages 104–105 and 124) which play an important role in the build-up of new land. Their tangled masses act like giant strainers that catch and hold sand, silt, and plant debris brought in by currents and tidal action, which later form soil.

It is interesting that the roots of certain plants (and probably also those of others so far still undiscovered) are known to release subtle poisons that slow down or prevent the growth of competing plants. Grass roots, for example, produce a substance that slows down the growth of apple trees, while the roots of black walnut trees exude a chemical compound that prevents many other plants from growing. A number of shrubs native to the arid American Southwest—for example guayule and creosote bush—release growth-inhibiting substances through their roots which effectively eliminate competitive plants; and eucalyptus trees inhibit nearly all ground cover, woody and herbaceous alike.

Another root oddity are the so-called "knees" of the bald cypress (see picture page 58), the breathing roots that project above the surface of the lake shallows which form the natural habitat of these trees. They enable the cypress trees, which grow in poorly aerated soil, to increase their oxygen intake.

Picture pages 101–113

101. Sequoia *(Sequoia gigantea)*. This photograph shows approximately one-quarter of the main root of a large sequoia that fell from natural causes a few years ago. Compare its size to that of the man sitting on it. The root system of these trees, including rootlets, can occupy an area larger than an acre. Yet despite this enormous lateral extent, sequoia roots are relatively shallow, forming a mat which rarely goes deeper than ten feet.

102. Fig tree *(Ficus* sp.). The aerial or *adventitious* roots that issue from its trunk and boughs, on reaching the ground, will augment the tree's regular root system and also serve as props for limbs.

103. Pandanus, or screw pine *(Pandanus veitchii)*. A palm-like tropical plant growing thirty to forty feet high, characterized by masses of prop roots, which, in addition to fulfilling the purpose of ordinary roots, tend to stabilize the top-heavy tree.

104–105. Mangrove *(Rhizophora mangle)*. The numerous prop roots make it appear as though the trees were crossing shallow water on stilts. This tropical tree is common along the shores and keys of southern Florida, where it forms miles of impenetrable thickets (see also picture page 124).

106–107. Strangler fig trees *(Ficus aurea)*. These are two stranglers whose original hosts are long since dead and gone. The power of their roots in search of water is almost beyond belief—splitting rocks, cracking concrete and masonry, lifting boulders inches from their beds. Such strength is evident in the crushing grip of the knotted roots that anchor them.

108–109. Banyan tree *(Ficus benghalensis)*. This whole immense structure is a single integrated tree. Starting life as an inconspicuous plant high up in a host tree where its seed had been left by a bird, the seedling banyan sends down aerial roots which penetrate the ground, gradually grow thick and strong, and eventually smother the host tree. These "trunks" in turn produce lateral extensions which again drop roots. By repeating this maneuver, with the aid of increasing numbers of adventitious roots which support its far-flung branches, a single banyan may grow into what looks like an entire grove, with hundreds of "trunks" and a ground coverage of more than an acre. Its diagonal struts and braces form a girder-like structure that rivals a bridge truss in soundness and solidity of construction.

110–111. Strangler fig *(Ficus aurea)*. This relative of the banyan also starts life as an epiphyte—a plant which grows on another plant without being parasitic on it. Like the banyan, it normally smothers its host, but unlike the former it produces only a single trunk. These photographs show this murderer's vise-like stranglehold on its victims.

112–113. European beech *(Fagus* sp.). These are the roots of trees that crashed to the shore from the height of Moens Klint in Denmark when parts of the cliff caved in, undercut by the battering action of the waves. Washed clean of earth and gravel, their intricate structure is laid bare, making it understandable why such small root systems can securely hold such large trees: imagine all the thousands of interstices tightly packed with soil and rock, and you get a solid mass weighing tons, well suited to counterbalance the weight of trunk and crown.

Thorns and spines have nothing to do with roots and are included here only for reasons of space. Although often used interchangeably, botanically speaking these two terms refer to different structures. *Thorns* are modified branches, sharp-pointed stems which may bear buds and leaves; they are found in honey locust, crab apple, Osage orange, and hawthorn. *Spines* are evolved from leaves which have lost their familiar flatness and have become slender, pointed, and hard; they are characteristic of black locust (whose spines are modified *stipules*, appendages that grow in pairs on each side of the base of the leaf of certain plants), barberry, and cacti. The "thorns" of rose and blackberry are, botanically speaking, *prickles*, structures which evolved neither from branches nor from leaves, but are merely outgrowths of superficial stem tissue.
The purpose of all these organs is, of course, defensive,

and what seems to me thought-provoking is that physically similar and functionally often identical structures have been evolved by many animals. Among those which carry such defensive spines are the hedgehog, porcupine, and spiny anteater; certain lizards and fishes; many insects, quite a few lobsters and crabs, a number of sea shells, and sea urchins and starfish. This "coincidence" is another proof of the relatedness of all things natural and the existence of basic principles which manifest themselves in identical ways, no matter whether they take animal or plant form.

Picture pages 114–116

Kapok *(Ceiba pentandra)*, sandbox tree *(Hura crepitans)*, and palm trunk *(Acrocomia* sp.). The defensive structures that occur in many forms as thorns, spines, and prickles may cover the fruit, leaves, leaf stalks, branches, or trunks. Here are some examples of the last variety. Their business-like efficiency should make any animal or man think twice before he attempts to climb one of these trees to pick their fruit.

88

101   102—103 ▶

XII
The Forest

A walk in the deep forest can be an experience as moving and memorable as exploring the sunken silence of the sea or listening to the murmur and thunder of the organ in a medieval cathedral. The forest envelops us from all sides with protective shelter. The upper reaches of the trees shut out the sky like a roof. The rising boles are columns holding up the vaulted dome. Subdued sunlight, filtered and colored by its passage through the canopy of leaves, like sunlight filtered through stained glass, quivers with the green shimmer of underwater light. The ceaseless hum of air moving through branches is as timeless as the wash of distant waves. In the presence of something as enormous and everlasting as the sea or the forest the brief span of our existence becomes more precious and meaningful.

A forest is more than trees. It is a complex system of mountains and valleys, hills and flats, dense thickets and rocky ravines, open glades carpeted with wild flowers, springs and creeks, bogs, lakes, and streams. It is a huge living organism whose components are specific plants and animals so adjusted to one another that they thrive together under similar conditions—an ecological unit called a *biota*. In this community of living things the most conspicuous members are, of course, the tall trees—oak and hickory, beech and maple, hemlock, spruce, and others. It is they who control the soil and the light and thereby determine which other plants and animals shall live in this particular forest. Below the canopy of the dominant trees lies the twilight zone of the smaller or understory trees—redbud, sassafras, blue beech, witch hazel, dogwood, and so forth. A rich variety of plants covers the forest floor—Solomon's seal and mayflower, jack-in-the-pulpit, trillium, mosses, and ferns. Living in and on the soil are fungi and bacteria. Lichens of various kinds and colors cling to trunks, branches, and rocks. Each type of forest houses a particular fauna—bear and badger, porcupine and deer, fox and racoon, skunk, squirrel, and mouse. Hawk and owl, grouse and dove, woodpecker, songbird, and chickadee. Snake, turtle, frog, and toad. A multitude of insects and spiders, centipedes and millipedes, snails and worms, each dependent for sustenance on others. There is activity in every nook and corner of the forest, a quivering and humming like that of a gigantic machine—and in a sense, a forest *is* a machine, a transformer of energy which forever converts the cosmic radiation of the sun into the substance of living plants and animals.

Sunlight beating down on the leaves of trees and plants is partly reflected or transmitted, partly dissipated in the form of heat, and partly used to power the processes of photosynthesis. Feeding on leaves, fruits, seeds or wood, herbivorous animals, seed- and berry-eating birds, and plant-eating insects and their larvae convert some of this plant material into animal tissues. Flesh-eating animals, insect-eating birds and birds of prey, snakes, frogs, toads, and carnivorous insects feed in turn on these vegetable eaters. Many of these flesh-eaters will in time fall prey to other predators—hawks eat snakes which eat frogs which eat ground beetles which eat caterpillars which eat leaves. In the end, of course, all animals and plants must die, but even their carcasses may give sustenance to scavengers and saprophytes (organisms which obtain their food from dead organic matter). Fungi and bacteria break down dead organic matter into simpler compounds, which sink into the ground, are taken up by plants through their roots, and, combining with food produced by photosynthesis powered by sunlight, take part in the growth of new plants. And the cycle of energy transfer begins again.

Organisms depending one on another in an eater-eaten relationship are said to form a *food chain*. The food chain always begins with green plants—the leaves, seeds, fruits and other parts of land plants; the phytoplankton of the sea. And generally, the end of each chain is formed by a large flesh-eater—lion, bear, and fox, hawks and large owls on land; sharks and whales in the sea. Some food chains are as long as or longer than the one from leaves to hawk cited above; others are short, such as the one in which antelopes eat grass and are in turn eaten by lions.

A healthy forest is a self-adjusting community of plants and animals in which each of the inhabitants gets its fair share of food and *Lebensraum.* Insects, diseases, or fire may temporarily interfere with the orderly unfolding of life processes within the community, but they are natural disturbances which the forest can overcome without permanent scars. True disaster strikes only when man intervenes and with clumsy hands tears some of the strands that form nature's complicated web. The drastic consequences that follow man's wholesale cutting of trees have already been described elsewhere. But similarly drastic results occur when the delicately adjusted balance of animal relationship is disturbed. The classic example of this is the case of the Kaibab deer. The Kaibab, a huge forest covering large parts of northern Arizona, was declared a national game preserve in 1906 by President Theodore Roosevelt. Deer hunting was prohibited, and in order to increase the size of the herds, game wardens set out systematically to destroy all the natural enemies of the deer. Within the next twenty years, over 6,000 mountain lions, wolves, coyotes, and bobcats were slain, with the result that the deer population, which had numbered around 4,000, grew by leaps and bounds until, by 1924, it had reached an all-time high of close to 100,000 does, bucks, and fawns. The inevitable result, of course, was mass starvation, since the range could not produce sufficient food to sustain the huge herds. After having eaten every available sapling and blade of grass, the population collapsed, and in two successive winters some 60,000 deer starved and froze to death. Because of man's interference, a healthy and stable deer population had first exploded and then collapsed; an entire range had suffered catastrophic damage from overgrazing and overbrowsing, with certain species of plants such as willows and raspberries all but eradicated, and the growth of young aspen halted for nearly twenty years; and the entire character of the biota was endangered to such a degree that, if deer ravage had continued, the forest would have given way to tree-dotted grassland.

Similar tragedies have occurred in many other parts of the country. Between 1910 and 1928 Pennsylvania's deer population increased from a few thousand to more than one million and then collapsed just like the Kaibab deer. In this case, the cause of the population explosion was a combination of predator extermination, establishment of large refuges, and an ironclad hunting law prohibiting the shooting of

does. In Colorado, where in the late 1930's and early 1940's deer had been fed in an attempt to tide them through the winter crisis, nearly half the fawns died on one canyon feeding ground. Comparable losses occurred on other feeding grounds, and after the snow had melted, game wardens working in one limited locality stacked up nearly 6,000 carcasses of dead deer out of sight of the highway, drenched them with oil, and lit the pyre. The range was capable of carrying a herd of 12,000 deer on a sustained basis, yet a census showed 23,400 deer, and the local people had been battling the laws against shooting does.

Quite a different lesson is to be learned from the rise, fall, and eventual stabilization of the moose population at Isle Royal National Park in Lake Superior. Moose first became established there in 1912 with the arrival of a few animals from the Canadian mainland who apparently had crossed the ice in search of food or in flight from wolves. In the presence of favorable conditions and the absence of predators, the moose multiplied prodigiously until the herd numbered more than 1,500 head. Then the food supply gave out, mass starvation set in, and by 1934 the moose population was down to a few hundred. The range recovered, and, as the food supply increased, the moose followed suit and their numbers again rose sharply. Then wolves migrated to the island and began to act as a check on the moose population. For several years now, the number of moose has been a stable 600, despite an annual increase of 160 calves. Obviously, the number of moose taken by the wolves—mostly animals enfeebled by age and disease—more or less balances the rate of growth. The number of moose is now in equilibrium with the carrying capacity of their range, and the animals are healthy and well fed. The wolves have likewise achieved a balance between their numbers and their food supply. And the forest is able to sustain both prey and predator and is in better shape than it was before the arrival of the wolves.

A particularly important group of forest dwellers are the insects, which usually make up in numbers what they lack in size. A few species can inflict enormous damage on trees; some are moderately harmful; others harmless, and many are indispensable for the orderly functioning of the forest community. Beneficial insects pollinate flowering plants, feed on countless numbers of harmful insects, and clean up waste products and organic remains. Together with the indifferent and the harmful insects, they also provide food for a large number of higher animals—notably shrews, racoons, skunks, snakes, toads, frogs, and insect-eating birds. The few truly destructive species of insects are the number one enemies of the trees, and their annual damage probably exceeds that of all forest fires combined.

Insects are indigenous members of the forest community, and under ordinary conditions the damage which harmful species do to trees is not very serious and must be accepted as normal—it is *endemic*. Periodically, however, conditions become extraordinarily favorable to the development of a particular insect species, which then increases its numbers out of all proportions to become *epidemic*.

The most destructive and widespread epidemics are those caused by several species of bark beetles and by the gypsy moth, the latter brought to the United States in 1869 by a French scientist who saw it as a potential producer of silk. Some of his specimens escaped and, in the absence of natural enemies, multiplied and spread, causing incalculable damage and now infesting an estimated 40 million acres of forest despite all efforts to eradicate or at least contain them. Insect epidemics are difficult to fight effectively because indiscriminate spraying of insecticides from aircraft also kills most of the beneficial insects, including the natural enemies of the pest, thereby seriously disrupting the ecological balance in the forest and often doing more harm than good. Campaigns based on the introduction (or increase in numbers) of the natural enemies of the respective pest seem much more promising, particularly when the destructive insect has been imported from abroad (usually accidentally) and has no natural enemies in its new habitat. Another method of pest control which avoids the use of poisonous chemicals consists of raising in captivity large numbers of males which are set free after first having been sterilized by radiation; they mate with females as freely as their "wild" untreated brothers but are infertile, and the subsequently laid eggs will not hatch. A third nonpoisonous type of pest control uses artificially synthesized male and female sex hormones of the respective species; these "natural" chemicals, whose scents are irresistible to members of the opposite sex, are then used to bait traps in which the captured insects perish.

Fire is the number two destroyer of trees. An account of the toll of our forests which fire takes year after year and how its ravages can be checked is in Chapter XVI. But although about 90 per cent of forest fires are caused by man, the remaining ten per cent are due to lightning—in other words, forest fires have been a common natural phenomenon since time immemorial. The black marks on the trunks of the sequoias on picture pages 98–99 are scars left by old forest fires, and studies of the growth rings of redwoods have shown that during the past thousand years fire swept these woods on the average of about four conflagrations per century. The "big trees" have survived so many forest fires because of their highly fire-resistant bark; actually, many of these fires probably had a mildly beneficial effect in clearing the forest floor of dense plant growth and debris, thereby providing potential seedling grounds. As a matter of fact, some species of trees—particularly aspen, jack pine, pitch pine, and lodgepole pine—depend to a large extent on forest fires for their survival; partly because they thrive best when fully exposed to sunlight, for young trees will not grow in the deep shade cast by dense old trees, and partly because the cones of these three species of pine usually remain tightly closed and will not release their seeds until heated by the flames of a light fire that has swept quickly through their stands. Actually, unopened jack pine cones often stay on the branches long enough to become embedded in the wood of the growing tree and eventually disappear from sight. Seeds extracted from such ingrown cones have been found viable even after many years. After a fire in a certain forest in Minnesota, where the number of jack pines per acre had been perhaps a dozen, thousands of new jack pine seedlings could be seen covering the ground.

After insects and fire, diseases rank third in order as destroyers of trees. According to national figures released by the United States Forest Service, insects and diseases together cause an estimated 21.2 billion board feet of *growth losses* of saw timber per year (this is the volume lost following pest attack due to deterioration of the stand or site). Insects cause an esti-

moss, is followed by sedges, cranberries and blue-berries, sheep laurel and heath, and ends with spruce and larch. The dominant trees of this region are spruce and fir; next in order are pine, larch, cedar, aspen, and birch.

The Pacific Coast Forest covers the western slopes of the Cascade Mountains in British Columbia, Washington, and Oregon and continues southward into California along the Pacific side of the Cascades and the Coast Range. The climate is mostly cool and moist; low clouds and fog are common; and precipitation in some areas exceeds 125 inches a year. This is perhaps the most magnificent forest in the entire world, a veritable fairyland of giant trees and tall ferns, moss-covered trunks and branches, with a rich undergrowth of smaller trees and herbaceous plants. The scale of the trees is awe-inspiring: in the northern part of the forest western hemlock and Douglas fir grow more than 200 feet tall with boles that measure six and eight feet in diameter. Farther south, the red-wood empire extends along the California coast from southern Monterey County northward over 500 miles to a point just across the Oregon border (see picture pages 76–80); finally, there are the giant sequoias (see picture pages 97–100). Other important trees of the Pacific coast forest are Sitka spruce, sugar and lodgepole pines, western red and incense cedar, and true firs. This forest produces almost one-third of United States lumber, about one-fifth of United States pulpwood, and nearly all of United States fir plywood.

The Rocky Mountain Forest, which produces about one-fourth of United States lumber, extends from the crest of the Cascade Mountains and the Coast Range on the west, to the eastern slopes of the Rocky Mountains, and from Canada on the north to Mexico on the south. Because the dominant trees are pines, this area is also known as the Western Pine Region. In Washington, Idaho, and Montana extensive areas are covered by western (Idaho) pine accompanied by western larch, western hemlock, red cedar, and white fir. But the dominant trees are the magnificent ponderosa (yellow) pine and Douglas fir, followed by sugar pine, Engelmann spruce, lodgepole pine, incense and western red cedar, and true firs. At their northern limit, ponderosa pines occur at altitudes of

3,000 feet, but in Arizona and New Mexico they thrive at 8,000 feet. As far as plants and animals are concerned, an ascent in altitude is equivalent to a move northward—an increase in elevation of 1,000 feet being the approximate equivalent of a 600-mile trip north. Beyond a certain altitude, trees can no longer exist because the climate is too harsh, no matter how near the equator. This frontier above which trees cannot grow is called the *timber line* and lies in the central part of the Rockies at approximately 11,000 feet (see picture pages 32–36).

The Northern (hemlock-hardwood) Forest, together with the Central Hardwood Forest and the Southern Forest, comprises the Eastern Forest Belt—the world's richest forest region in the temperate zone, containing some 600 species of trees. It covers an area that extends from Minnesota through northern Wisconsin and Michigan northeastward to the coast of Maine, with a long, narrow extension running southward along the mountain chains across the New England states, New York, and Pennsylvania, through West Virginia and Tennessee into northern Georgia. It produces about one-tenth of United States lumber and almost one-fifth of United States pulpwood. Dominant trees are red and white pine, jack pine, spruce, and fir. The shores and surrounding lowlands of its many lakes and bogs are often ringed with white cedar, larch (tamarack), and spruce. In abandoned fields and burned areas, aspen and paper birch are abundant. Eastern hemlock intermixed with beech, maple, basswood (linden), yellow birch, and other hardwoods thrives in the more fertile valleys.

The Central Hardwood Forest extends from the Great Plains west of the Mississippi to the Atlantic and from the Northern Forest almost to the Gulf of Mexico, partly split by the thin strip of Northern Forest that covers the Appalachian Mountain range. The climate is moderate and precipitation averages forty to fifty inches a year, resulting in luxuriant vegetation and rich, deep soil. This is a largely decidu-ous forest whose dominant trees are beech, oak, red maple, hickory, elm, ash, walnut, sycamore, tulip tree, black and sweet gum, Virginia and shortleaf pine, and red cedar. This forest produces about one-twentieth of United States lumber and almost one-tenth of United States pulpwood.

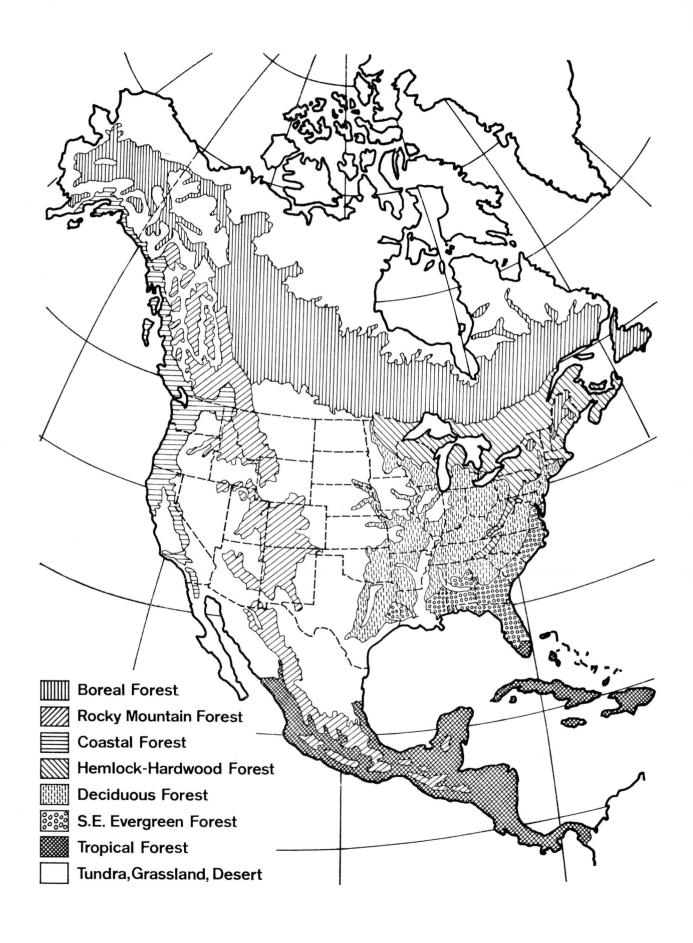

Boreal Forest
Rocky Mountain Forest
Coastal Forest
Hemlock-Hardwood Forest
Deciduous Forest
S.E. Evergreen Forest
Tropical Forest
Tundra, Grassland, Desert

The Southern Forest covers a narrow belt along the Atlantic and Gulf coasts, extending from New Jersey to eastern Texas. It is the source of nearly one-third of United States lumber, more than three-fifths of United States pulpwood, and large quantities of turpentine and other resin products. A typical feature is its hot, dry, sandy pine barrens where loblolly, shortleaf, longleaf, and slash pine are dominant. In the rich soil of the bottom lands, live oak, red and black gum, magnolia, hickory, and pecan are prevalent. Other outstanding features of this region are the rootless "Spanish moss" that festoon the branches of live oak and cypress (see picture pages 52–56) and the creeping saw palmettos that form immense matted tangles among the sandhill pines. Sluggish muddy rivers cross the coastal plains and produce extensive swamps and backwaters overgrown with impenetrable jungles of bald cypress (see picture page 58) and coast white cedar, although large specimens of these are trees nowadays rare.

The Tropical Forest touches the continental United States only at the southern tip of Florida and in a small area of southeastern Texas, often in the form of hammocks—comparatively small areas covered by an unbelievably dense and lush growth of broadleaved evergreens including palms, strangler figs, and, in the Everglades, one species of mahogany (see picture pages 3, 92–96, 102–111). Many coastal areas and almost all of the "keys"—the small islands southeast of Florida—are edged by extensive mangrove thickets (see picture pages 104–105 and 124) which form one of the strangest and most impenetrable of all forests. The enmeshed arching roots of these shrub-like trees rise directly out of the salt water and seem to carry the often horizontal "trunks" on stilts. Photographs showing most of the types of forest mentioned in this chapter can be found on the following picture pages: the Boreal Forest, picture page 4; the Pacific Coast Forest, picture pages 76–80, 97–100; the Rocky Mountain Forest, picture page 1; the Northern Forest, picture pages 142–143; the Southern Forest, picture page 58; the Tropical Forest, picture pages 14 and 124. Some of the more extreme and unusual tree habitats are shown on the picture pages that follow.

Picture pages 117–124

117. Mixed spruce-fir forest in the Canadian Northwest. These trees have advanced as far as they can go, right up to the edge of the Columbia Icefield, where they were stopped by the lateral moraine of the Athabaska glacier. Beyond this point nothing can live among the rock, snow, ice, eternal gales, and bone-chilling cold.

118–119. Dead conifers in Yellowstone National Park. Everywhere on earth, life penetrates to the very edge of death—to the point beyond which conditions make living impossible. These trees had overstepped the boundary and were killed by steam and the poisonous solutions from a nearby geyser.

120–121. Saguaro *(Carnegiea gigantea)*. A cactus is not a tree but a nonwoody plant. Nevertheless, I included these because they are big, beautiful, and unique, and visitors to the American Southwest cannot fail to notice their spectacular forms. Saguaros, which grow to fifty feet, are the largest cacti on earth. They are found only in Arizona, New Mexico, southern California, and the Sonoran Desert in Mexico. Unfortunately, the days of the giant saguaros may be numbered because they are gradually succumbing to a virus.

122–123. These western pines standing forlornly in a desolate landscape are the forerunners of a new forest. The scene is California's Lassen Volcanic Park where an eruption of the cindercone in the background buried the previous forest under mountains of flaming lava and hot volcanic ash. But life is irrepressible, and the ground had barely time to cool before new seeds were blown in by the wind and trees began to sprout. Soon the forest will re-establish itself.

124. Mangrove *(Rhizophora mangle)*. This is the edge of a mangrove swamp in southern Florida; the trees, rising out of the briny sea on their arching stilt-like roots, form one of the most impenetrable forests on earth.

XIII
Wood

Wood is composed of various types of cells. These cells, most of which are strongly elongated, form an intricate, three-dimensional arrangement of vertical tube-like cells called *tracheids* and horizontal cells forming so-called *vascular rays* (or *pith rays*) which radiate from the vicinity of the pith (tissue occupying the center of the trunk or branch) into the *phloem* (the thin layer of cells between wood and bark through which soluble foods are conducted). Together, these two types of cells form an interconnected system of pipelines through which water and nutritious solutions can be transported both vertically and laterally throughout the tree. As the tree grows and its trunk and branches increase in girth, the cells of the inner wood layers, the *heartwood*, gradually become infiltrated by gums, resins, tannins, and other complex organic compounds, often darken in color, and die; only the *sapwood*, the outer ring of lighter colored wood between the heartwood and the bark, contains live cells. Structural differences make it advisable to distinguish between two different types of wood with different properties: softwood and hardwood.

Softwood, or coniferous wood, is the wood of our cone-bearing evergreens—pine, fir, hemlock, redwood, spruce, etc. Softwood is characterized by tracheids which serve a double purpose: to provide a system of tubes to conduct water from the roots to the leaves, and to act as a supporting skeleton that gives the tree rigidity. As their name implies, softwoods are generally softer than hardwoods, *but there are exceptions:* the "hardwoods" poplar, basswood, and balsa wood, for instance, are considerably softer than some "softwoods," such as certain kinds of cypress, juniper, and pine. The *true* difference between softwoods and hardwoods lies, therefore, *not* in the actual degree of softness or hardness but in structural characteristics.

Softwoods account for approximately 80 per cent of all the lumber used in the United States, a proportion that has remained more or less unchanged over the past forty years. In 1963, Western pine accounted for 29.2 per cent of total United States lumber production, Douglas fir for 23.3, Southern pine for 16.8, redwood for 6.3, and other softwoods for 4.2 per cent. Softwood burns much faster than hardwood and is excellent for kindling but normally unsuitable for firewood because it throws hot sparks that may ignite nearby combustible materials.

Hardwood, or dicotyledonous wood, is the wood of our Northern deciduous trees (oak, hickory, beech, etc.) and of Southern broad-leaved evergreens such as live oak, magnolia, fig, etc. Structurally, it differs from softwood insofar as the only function of its tracheids is to conduct sap; other cells, the *wood fibers*, provide mechanical rigidity (in softwoods, both functions are combined in the tracheids). Most (but not all) hardwoods are harder and heavier than softwoods. The heaviest, black ironwood *(Krugiodendron ferreum)*, is so heavy that it does not float, having a specific gravity of up to 1.49 and weighing as much as ninety-two pounds per cubic foot. The lightest wood is that of a Cuban tree *(Aeschynomene hispida)* which has a specific gravity of 0.044 and weighs only $2^3/_4$ pounds per cubic foot. By comparison, balsa wood, which varies considerably in density, weighs between $2^1/_2$ and 24 pounds per cubic foot while the average weight of cork is 15 pounds per cubic foot. The "hard" types of hardwood—hickory, maple, oak, etc.—make excellent firewood; they burn slowly, do not throw sparks, and leave a long-lasting bed of hot coals. "Softer" kinds of hardwood, such as poplar, willow, basswood, and black birch, burn much faster and are less desirable as fuel.

Annual growth rings in wood. Trees in the temperate zone grow in spurts: when climatic conditions are favorable—in spring, summer, and early fall—they increase their substance by producing new layers of cells; when temperatures are low, days short, or the water supply inadequate, cell production slows down or stops entirely. As a result of these variations in the rate of growth, wood is not homogenous but consists of concentric layers which can be clearly seen in the cross-section of any tree trunk, larger branch, or log of firewood. Because normally each layer or ring represents a single year's growth, these rings are called the *annual growth rings* of the tree.

Lateral growth—growth in girth—takes place only in the *cambium*, the thin layer of cells between the phloem and the wood. Here, each spring, new cells with large cavities and thin walls form a new layer of wood which, in the trunk, has the shape of an irregular hollow cone.

Later in the season this is followed by a second layer of somewhat smaller and denser cells. As a result, each annual growth ring comprises an inner layer, the early or spring wood, and an outer layer, the late or summer wood. These growth rings can best be seen in cross-sections of softwood, where the spring wood appears as a lighter and softer ring than the summer wood. In hardwoods, the diameters of the tracheids of the spring wood are larger than those of the summer wood. This can be seen clearly on picture page 128, which shows a cross-section through a piece of oak; the elongated black spots are the open-end cells of the tracheids; the more or less horizontally running light streaks are the pith rays. The number of growth rings between the pith and the cambium is equal to the age in years of the respective section of the tree. Since a tree grows in height as well as in girth, it is obvious that the number of annual growth rings varies with the height from the ground at which they are counted. Only a ring count made close to the ground (for instance, at the surface of the stump of a felled tree) will produce an accurate account of the tree's age although, occasionally, *false growth rings* may result in a figure that is somewhat too high; such extra rings are formed when tree growth is temporarily slowed down during a growth period, by severe drought or large-scale defoliation by insects, for example.

Because of variations in the factors which influence the growth of trees, the width of the annual growth rings is usually not uniform, and their sizes, shapes, and relation to one another contain a considerable amount of information about many incidents in the life of the particular tree; this "report" can be "read" by specialists. For example, broad, evenly spaced rings are indicative of favorable growing conditions—good soil, long growing season, plentiful water supply, and freedom from competition by other trees for water and light. Under such circumstances, in certain kinds of trees individual rings may be an inch wide. On the other hand, the more narrowly spaced the rings, the harsher the growing conditions—long cold winters

and correspondingly short growing seasons, poor soil, inadequate water supply due to unfavorable location or drought. Under such circumstances a tree may grow less than $1/100$ inch per year. However, it is a perfectly normal feature of a tree's senescence to produce relatively narrow rings during its later years; a sapling standing not thirty feet away may for the same year make a substantial addition to its xylem mass. The slowest growth rate ever recorded in a North American tree is that of a limber pine from Sun Valley, Idaho, which for a time increased in girth by only 0.118 inch (3 mm) *per century*. An abrupt change in the width of the annual growth rings is a sure sign of a sudden change in the conditions under which the respective tree grew. An abrupt *decrease* in the width of successive annual rings is, of course, indicative of a sudden worsening of growing conditions, and a sudden *increase* in ring width may signify a particularly long growing season with plenty of rain, or removal of competition from neighboring trees due to cutting or elimination by some natural cause. Fires also leave their mark indelibly engraved in the wood of a surviving tree and thus can be accurately dated, as those in the redwood and sequoia forests have been. Even such events as windstorms, landslides, and other violent disturbances can often be dated accurately by studying the annual rings in trees that have been tipped by them: leaning trees form rings that are eccentric. In conifers, such rings are abnormally wide in the portion near the lower side of the trunk, whereas most (but not all) hardwoods react to tipping in the opposite manner.

So revealing and reliable are the coded data of annual growth rings that they form the foundation for an entire new science: dendrochronology and climatology based on large-scale statistical tree-ring analysis. Pioneer work in this field has been done by the late Dr. Edmund Schulman and his assistant, Dr. C. W. Ferguson, of the Laboratory for Tree-Ring Research, University of Arizona, Tucson. Their intensive studies of long-lived trees in the arid regions of the American Southwest, and particularly of bristlecone pines (see picture pages 33–36), have resulted in the establishment of a "calendar" that goes back more than 6,600 years. This calendar enables archaeologists to date remnants of ancient civilizations accurately and provides climatologists with a complete record of the respective region's precipitation. To get first-hand information about this interesting subject, I interviewed Dr. Ferguson, who took me on a tour through the Laboratory of Tree-Ring Research, showed me the work currently done, and told me the following fascinating story:

Some twenty-five years ago, Dr. A. E. Douglass, in the course of climatic research at the University of Arizona, found that certain species of trees, particularly the Rocky Mountain Douglas fir and some other pines, showed marked variations in the width of their annual growth rings; these variations clearly were related to variations in precipitation: in a dry year, a narrow ring was formed; in an average year, a ring of average width resulted; and in a wet year, the ring was abnormally wide. Hence, by examining the wood of a representative sample of trees, the year-to-year climate of the region in question could be established as far back as the age of the oldest tree. So the next logical step was to hunt for very old trees.

This was the task which Dr. Schulman set himself, a task in which he was spectacularly successful: it was he who, in the bristlecone pines, discovered the oldest living things on earth. The age of any tree can be established without the need for cutting down the tree, by taking a *core sample* with an increment borer—a drill equipped with a hollow, tube-like bit that extracts a rod-like core of wood that extends from the bark to the pith. Such a core contains, of course, a sample of every growth ring of the tree. After extraction, the specimen, which is thinner than a pencil, is glued to a grooved stick for support, shaved down, polished, stained to intensify the often microscopically narrow growth rings, and studied under a microscope.

Working with cores extracted from living trees, Dr. Schulman and his co-workers were able to compile a complete climatological record that extended back more than 4,000 years. In the course of this work, they found that the same easily recognizable combinations of wider and narrower rings occurred in many trees, indicating specific climatic cycles that took place over certain periods of time, the accurate dates of which could be established by counting the number of annual rings from the bark (the present) back to the beginning of the significant ring pattern. By matching these revealing patterns of wider or narrower rings in the inner parts of very old trees

with identical patterns in timbers found in prehistoric Indian ruins, Dr. Ferguson was able not only to extend his "calendar" more than 6,600 years into the past, but also to establish precisely the dates at which the beams of these ancient pueblos had been cut. How this method of crossdating works is illustrated diagrammatically below:

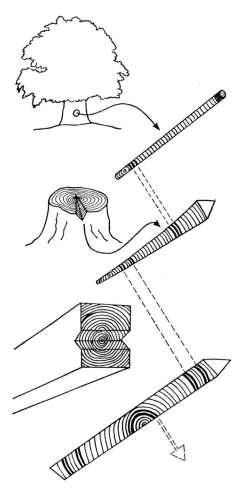

Thus, by decoding the information contained in wood—living as well as long since dead—scientists are able to "read" the message of the trees. They know now which years were particularly wet or dry. They found out that in 1290 a catastrophic twenty-four-year drought hit the American Southwest, and they now have reason to believe that this drought caused the sudden abandonment of the ancient cliff dwellings and pueblos in that region. No one can predict what other interesting facts may be revealed through further studies of trees.

Picture pages 125–140

125. What at first appears to be a carving—the caricature of a face—reveals itself as a natural growth, a piece of wood from a dead tree which I picked up from the forest floor and photographed.

126. The stump of a "hardwood" tree—an American elm in Brookfield, Connecticut, which succumbed to the Dutch elm disease and was chopped down in the fall of 1961. The life history of this approximately ninety-five-year-old tree is recorded in the pattern of its annual growth rings.

127. Close-up of "softwood." This is part of the eroded surface of an old white pine stump whose softer spring wood has weathered at a more rapid rate than the harder summer wood, causing the individual growth rings to stand out in bold relief.

128. Magnified cross-section of a piece of oak covering nine years' growth. In this picture, the annual growth rings run from right to left. The elongated black dots are the open-end cells of the tracheids of the spring wood, which are larger than those of the denser summer wood. The more or less horizontal white strips are pith rays.

129. Annual growth rings in poplar wood. Resembling strata of sedimentary rock, these layers of wood illustrate how the same process—in this case accretion—produces similar structures, no matter how unrelated the affected substances.

130. Eroded piece of "softwood." Weathering brought out the beautiful texture of the wood by exposing its natural "grain."

131. A knot in pine wood—the emergence of a branch from the trunk. Weathering reveals the internal structure of this junction and shows how the lateral growth of the branch is partly enveloped by the vertical growth of trunk wood.

132–133. Comparison between the modes of branching of red oak (left) and copper beech (right). Note how the oak's bark is wrinkled whereas that of the beech stays smooth.

134–135. Branching in American beech (*Fagus grandifolia.*) The trunks of old specimens are often magnificently sculptured and beautifully detailed, offering endless opportunities for discovery and enjoyment. Such trees should be studied—and explored by touch—like sculpture.

136–137. Dead branches of pinyon pine (*Pinus edulis*). Weathering reveals the fibrous nature of the wood of these tough little trees, wich are adapted to extremes of heat and cold. These photographs were made near the rim of the Grand Canyon.

138–140. Dead trees in Rocky Mountain National Park, Colorado. As a leafless tree reveals more about its structure than the same tree in foliage, so a dead and barkless trunk can demonstrate features invisible in the living tree. Here, the hulks of burned and weatherbeaten western spruce and pines reveal the twist that is typical of many trees but rarely visible while the bark is still on. The reason for this spiraling growth is unknown.

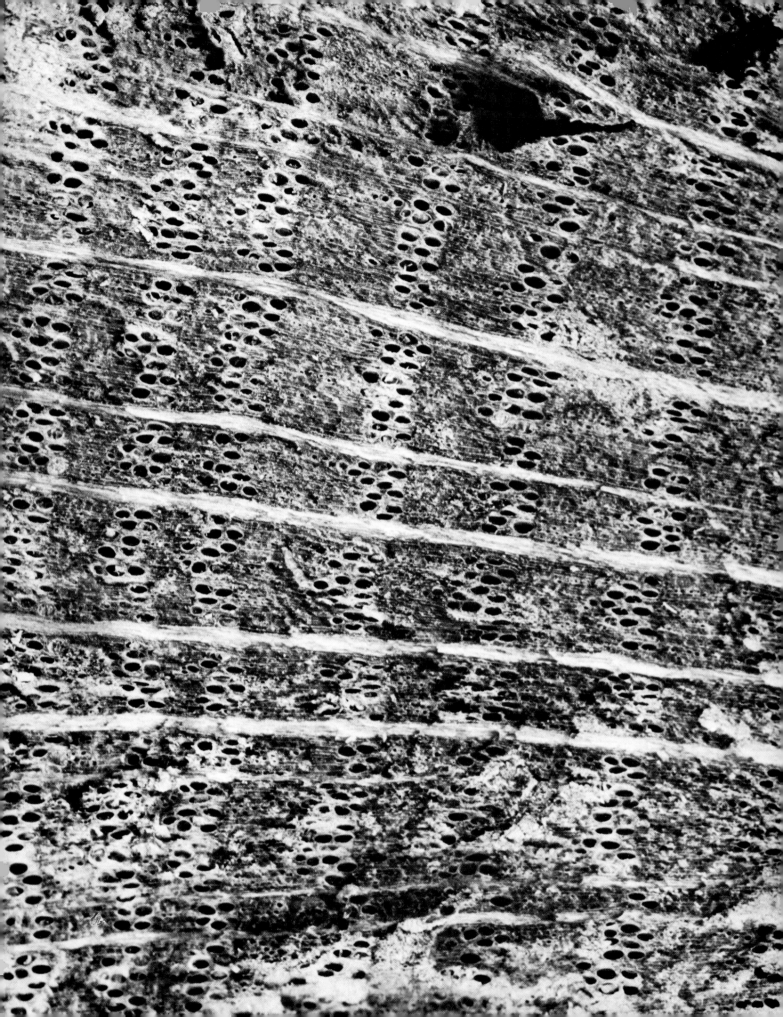

XIV
Fall Colors

Each autumn, before the winter dormancy, the hardwood forests of North America put on a spectacular parting performance—they change their color. Imperceptibly at first, then faster and faster, the familiar greens give way to all the hues of a sunset sky untill the entire landscape is aglow. The maples are usually the first to turn; driving to work one cool morning in fall one notices that the green of familiar trees is dappled with orange, like giant brushes dipped gently into cans of yellow, orange, or red paint. A few days later, the color spots have multiplied, and the branches now have incandescent tips. Another week goes by and all the maples seem aflame. Gradually other trees light up: birches and poplars glow in golden hues, oaks burn red and purple, sweet gums are scarlet flames, and aspens are riots of yellow. Newspapers advise where the most spectacular color displays are, and every weekend droves of New Englanders take to the woods for one last breath of clean air and one last look at living color before the gray curtains of rain and fog close the show for the winter.

The brilliant color displays which many deciduous trees put on each fall is the result of adaptation to our northern winters. As the days get shorter and the light of the lower-riding sun becomes less powerful, photosynthesis slows down, and changes occur in the chemistry of the leaf. When frost finally begins to lock up the water supply of the tree, leaves become useless or worse—potential wasters of precious water through evaporation—and are discarded. But before they fall, the production of chlorophyll, the light-sensitive green pigment, ceases. And as the chlorophyll content of the leaf diminishes, other pigments that were already there but masked by chlorophyll begin to shine through. These are primarily the carotenoids and the anthocyanins.

Carotenoid pigments are the coloring matter of yellow flowers, fruits, and autumn leaves. They are known to be a source of vitamin A for animals and are suspected of playing a role in effecting the phototropic (light-induced) movements of plants. They have been found in more than sixty different plant-manufactured compounds and produce a variety of colors that range from lemon yellow to orange. Beyond this, very little is known about these pigments except the probably meaningless fact that they are extremely persistent. As a matter of fact, they are so indestructible that they cannot be broken down by the digestive juices of animals—the yellow color of butter and egg yolks is caused by carotenoids which cows and hens have ingested.

Anthocyanins are plant-produced pigments that range in color from pale pink through red to purple and blue. They give red apples, many flowers, and autumn leaves their brilliant hues. Whatever other functions these pigments may fulfill is, however, not known at present.

Leaves are rather fragile structures. They furthermore furnish food for armies of caterpillars, leaf miners, and other hungry denizens of the forest; by the end of summer an unmutilated leaf is a rarity. By annually shedding their leaves deciduous trees gain another advantage over evergreens: they can start each spring with a new set of leaves. Evergreens, incidentally, also shed and regrow their needles, or leaves, but at no time is the tree entirely bare, thus always appearing green.

The start of the annual fall color display is brought about by changes in light intensity and temperature. Production of anthocyanins is stimulated by light—the well-exposed outermost leaves of a tree are always more brilliantly colored than the more shaded leaves deep within the crown. Bright and sunny fall weather is therefore more conducive to colorful leaf displays than overcast skies and rain. Contrary to widespread belief, frost does not affect the color of leaves, and some of the most brilliant autumn color displays occur before the onset of frost, provided that temperatures generally have been low.

Picture pages 141–144

141. A shagbark hickory leaf, transfigured by the weak October sun, lights up and shines like hammered gold before its final fall.

142–143. A mixed hemlock-hardwood forest in the

Adirondacks, New York. These are the pensive colors of fall—pinks and purples cooled by a bluish haze that like a thin veil of smoke hangs over valleys and peaks. Skies are cloudy, rain is in the air, the higher elevations are already white with frost, which will melt as the sun breaks through. What was a sea of green only a month ago is now an ocean of reds—like the image of a forest photographed on infrared film.

144. A red maple in full autumn glory. Sweet gum, sumac, and aspen may approach it, but no tree surpasses its burning intensity of brilliant color: sugar maples turn yellow and orange, red maples scarlet and wine red—the richest, brightest, most colorful foliage in the world.

XV
European Trees

Since time immemorial, man has seen trees as symbols, investing them with magic powers, assigning specific forces to specific trees. The world-ash Yggdrasill was a symbol of the universe; Christmas is still incomplete without a Christmas tree; orange blossoms accompany wedding bells; laurels reward the victor. Mimosa is the symbol of shyness and virginity, the olive branch the sign of peace. We say "stout as an oak," we call a graceful dancer "willowy," and tough old Andrew Jackson was affectionately known as "Old Hickory."

In a sense, this tree symbolism also extends to countries. The oak, for example, has always been a symbol of Germany; olive trees typify Italy or Greece; redwoods suggest California; live oak is the tree of the American South; palms make us think of tropical island shores. And so it occurred to me that, perhaps, other kinds of trees might be characteristic of other countries—for example, typical French or Danish trees. The last time I was in Europe I sought "typical" trees, and here is what I found:

Picture pages 145–160

145. Plane trees in the Jardin des Plantes, Paris. The French love of ornamentation and decorative design extends also to trees, and as I traveled through France it seemed to me that Frenchmen were congenitally unable to let any tree develop naturally. The result of this obsession with saw and pruning shears can be admired not only in the formal gardens of Versailles and other French *châteaux*, but in every town and village and along virtually every highway of France. The plane trees shown in this picture have been *pollarded*, i.e., cut back repeatedly to promote the development of a dense head of foliage and to bring them in line with the linear layout of the park. The result is rather spectacular, interesting when the trees bare their skeletal structure, useful when they are in foliage because shade is intensified, and typically French.

146–147. Trees bordering the Seine in Paris. One of the qualities that makes Paris not only great and unique but human and lovable is her enormous wealth of trees. A stroll among the horse-chestnuts and sycamores that border the Champs Elysées on a warm evening in spring, when the light from the street lamps twinkles through the still translucent leaves, is an unforgettable experience. Nor will a visitor ever forget the magnificent old trees that stand along the embankments of the Seine—the poplars (picture page 146) with their massive trunks and arching limbs, and the plane trees (picture page 147) whose dangling "button balls" write music in the sky. Their rising forms effectively counterbalance the severe horizontal French architecture, and their green canopy of leaves provides shade for the browsers among the bookstalls on sunny summer afternoons.

148. A *Hainbuche*—a European cousin of our beech—in Nymphenburger Park, Munich, Germany. The powerful design of the bark with its alternating bands of rough and shiny green make this beautiful German tree easy to recognize.

149. The trunk of a London plane in Geneva, Switzerland. The bark of this relative of our sycamore flakes off in rounded chips, producing the effect of a three-dimensional geological relief map. Originally a native of Europe, this tree, because of its resistance to polluted air, is nowadays planted widely as a street tree in all the major cities of the temperate zones.

150. Beeches at Moens Klint, Denmark. These wind-driven trees at the very edge of Denmark's famous beech forests fight a losing rear-guard battle with the sea. Standing at the brink of the precipice (which is shown from a different angle on picture page 160), they are doomed to perish as the relentless waves undermine the cliff and from time to time cause huge masses of rocks and trees to crash down to the beach. When spring comes to Denmark, its beech forests become one of the wonders of the world. Nothing comparable exists anywhere (see picture pages 5 and 81). The trees with their beautiful silvery bark are widely spaced, giving the woods a feeling of airy openness that is further enhanced by the sparseness of the delicate foliage. Transluminated by the sun, myriads of young leaves form diaphanous clouds of the sheerest

and brightest green around the network of black branches. But perhaps the most charming feature of Denmark's spring woods are the millions of anemones and buttercups that cover the forest floor in solid sheets of white and yellow, making the visitor hesitate to set foot on this enchanted carpet.

151. A weeping beech in Schleswig, Germany. Spooky and weird, its wildly convoluted branches make this tree appear like a witch's home in some magic woods.

152–153. The plane trees of Moulins, France. Like revelers joining hands at a ring dance, these pollarded trees will soon form massive walls of shade for the citizens of this sleepy town. Pollarding is an art in which the French are masters, and the results of their labors can be seen in almost any town from Paris to Carcassonne in the form of magnificently styled old trees admirably fitted into often very cramped spaces, providing welcome shade to markets and streets.

154. A French country road—a *chaussée*—lined by pollarded plane trees. Unlike Americans, who see in every tree a hazard to automobile traffic, the French have a sufficiently great love for trees to accept such risks as worth while. At the moment, this *chaussée* looks as if bordered by shell-damaged pillars. But a few years hence, after the "roof" has grown, it will be a magnificent green tunnel. Tree-lined roads such as this are as common in France as they are unthinkable in America.

155. Pollarded French roadside trees. People living in neighboring villages periodically trim these trees to induce them to grow large quantities of tough thin branches, the raw material for their broom home industry.

156. European willows. Hollow old trees such as these are typical of northwestern Germany, Holland, and many parts of France. They are pollarded year after year to provide a dense crop of shoots suitable for making baskets.

157. Lombardy poplars near Macon, France. This is one of the most typical French roadside trees. The multitudinous thin branches hugging the trunk grow upward naturally. This is a relative of our cottonwood, the tree planted as a windbreak, the shelter-belt tree of our prairie states.

158–159. Ancient oaks in Dyrehaven near Klampenborg, Denmark. Altogether, perhaps a dozen of these venerable trees survive. Their location in one of the hunting parks and game preserves of the former kings of Denmark saved them from the ax. Their gnarled trunks are hoary with age, misshapen, moss-covered, looking more like rocks than bark and wood. Yet each spring myriads of bright young leaves issue from their knotty branches, their sprightly green incongruous with the decaying appearance of these battered hulks.

160. Beeches at Moens Klint, Denmark. This is literally "land's end," where Europe's most famous beech forest meets the Baltic sea. Like legions going into battle, the trees march right up to the edge of the precipice while their adversary, the waves, endlessly pounds and attacks from below. From time to time, sections of the cliff cave in, hurtling the trees into the sea. But the supply of trees is endless, and the struggle between the forest and the sea goes on eternally.

145   146–147 ▶

152

XVI
You Can Help

The right to own implies the duty to conserve. This moral axiom is nowhere more true than in regard to the trees and soil on which we all depend. It applies to all of us, from government agencies and industry to private citizen.

The total forest area of the United States, including Alaska and Hawaii, is some 759 million acres. Of these, approximately 509 million are classified as commercial and 250 million as noncommercial. Commercial forests are those from which timber harvests are available; noncommercial forest lands are either incapable of commercial timber production or have been set aside for wilderness, game refuges, parks, military installation, and other such uses. Of the commercial forest area, some 113 million acres are owned by the federal government; approximately 29 million acres by state and local governments; some 67 million acres by industry; and about 300 million acres are farm wood lots or otherwise privately owned.

Ownership of the forests of the United States is diversified, and this diversification naturally produces conflicts of interest. The farmer and small wood lot owner understandably want to keep out trespassing vacationers who trample the vegetation and dump their picnic trash on his land. Timberland owners are justifiably afraid that careless campers, hikers, or hunters might set their woods on fire. Lumber interests lobby incessantly for a greater share of the National Forests' timber crop and wage a never ending war with conservationists, who fight just as energetically to keep the government-owned forests—*their* forests—inviolate.

Fortunately, most people realize that the best anyone can hope for is some state of peaceful coexistence. This, of course, means compromise. Accordingly, most of the industry-owned forest lands, although managed primarily for production of timber crops, are now open to the public for hunting, fishing, and other recreation. According to figures published by the American Forest Products Industries, Inc., 92.3 per cent of these privately owned lands are open to hunters during the hunting season, and 97.4 per cent, containing a total of some 37,000 miles of streams and 735,000 acres of lakes, are open to fishermen. In addition, more than a hundred lumber companies have developed some 300 public parks on their forest lands. Some of these parks are even equipped with free overnight facilities and such services as campgrounds and sanitary installations, camp stoves, tables and benches, and other conveniences that make fishing, boating, and swimming more enjoyable for vacationers who are not used to the rugged life of the woods.

In exchange for these privileges, the landowners expect their guests to respect their property. A good relationship between both parties, without which such privileges might be withdrawn, will be promoted if every visitor scrupulously observes the rules of good woodsmanship as drawn up by the Wilderness Society and reprinted in essence below:

"Take nothing but pictures; leave nothing but footprints" is a motto of the experienced camper or hiker which everyone should emulate and which children should be taught the first time they set foot in the woods. Littering a trail, leaving a dirty campsite, or befouling a stream or lake are unpardonable.

Always be careful with fire in the woods. Avoid smoking while traveling along a trail. When you do smoke, find a safe place, sit down, and relax for a while. Break and hold matches until cold before throwing them away. Crush cigarettes out on a rock and bury cigarette butts and pipe heels in mineral soil. Never forget that a runaway campfire can cause a holocaust that may destroy thousands of acres of forest. The experienced camper locates his campfires in safe places on rocks or mineral soil, out of the wind and away from trees and shrubs. He keeps his fires small, taking care to *put them out cold*, preferably with water.

Take pride in leaving your campsite spotless. Burn combustible refuse and pack up the cans, glass, foil, and other unburnables. Bury human wastes (a garden trowel will help with this method of waste disposal). Soap or detergent should be used in a pan, not put into streams or lakes. Try to dispose of wash water in a rocky area where drainage will not reach nearby plants. Clean fish and game away from campsites and waterfront.

Do not attempt to feed wild animals—especially bear or deer—no matter how friendly their appearance. Do

105

not approach them too closely. Never get between a mother bear and her cubs. "Plinking" at chipmunks, songbirds, and other wildlife is illegal as well as contemptible.

If everybody abides by these rules, the person who follows in our footsteps will never know we were there, and he will enjoy his trip as much as we did ours. If you wish to contribute more actively to the preservation of the beauty of our country, you have many opportunities to do so. Here are a few suggestions:

Teach your children to respect all living things, animals and plants, no matter how humble or small. As soon as they are old enough, give them a simple microscope for Christmas and make them aware of the beauty of the inconspicuous—the design in the wing of a butterfly, the iridescent sheen of a beetle's carapace, the convolutions of a snail. Encourage them to watch and study animals—starting with birds at the feeder, chipmunks and squirrels in the park, or caterpillars and butterflies in a cage. Where possible, take them regularly to the zoo, botanical garden, or arboretum, and later on trips into the woods. Teach them the use of binoculars, notebook, and identification guide. Let them join the Boy Scouts, the Girl Scouts, or the Camp Fire Girls. If you start your program early enough, you will never have to worry that your children may later become litterbugs or join the sorry society of people who carve their initials into trees or indolently stand by while others despoil the countryside. And no matter what they do after they grow up, you will have given them something precious to enrich their lives forever.

Let your voice be heard. You are a citizen, a voter, and a taxpayer, and as such you can make your voice carry weight. How often do you read or hear about something that makes your blood boil and think: This is too much, why doesn't somebody do something to stop it? The occasion may be relatively small, restricted to the community level, such as the cutting down of big old trees to make space for a new "development"; or it may be large and of nation-wide interest, such as the proposed dam that would back up the waters of the Colorado River into the Grand Canyon. These are the instances where every voice counts. Although the instigator of the particular outrage may be a commission or the government, let us not forget that commissions and governments are only groups of people,

public servants sensitive to public opinion, elected by a majority of people to serve the needs of all. And if a sufficiently large number object, the chances are that the offensive project will be modified or abandoned. Don't think your voice is too small or your vote too insignificant. Write to the planning commission, your councilman, your congressman, or send a telegram to the President himself if you feel that the occasion requires stronger measures! This is the meaning—and the opportunity—of freedom.

Join a conservation organization. To give your voice additional weight, become a member of one of America's great conservation societies. You will receive information periodically on the latest problems and achievements in conservation, enjoy a number of special privileges, and your membership dues will help support and expand an organization which, under the leadership of dedicated men and women, can do much more for the preservation of our national heritage than an equal number of individual unorganized citizens. Each of the six societies listed in alphabetical order below has its own program and offers specific advantages which are briefly described in excerpts from their respective prospectus:

National Audubon Society, Audubon House, 1130 Fifth Avenue, New York, New York 10028. Founded in 1905, the National Audubon Society is among the oldest and largest national conservation organizations in North America. Its major purpose is to advance public understanding of the value and need of conservation of wildlife, plants, soil, and water, and the relation of their intelligent treatment and wise use to human progress. This society protects forty-three different areas of land and water as wildlife sanctuaries. These range in size from small, offshore islands to one 26,000-acre block of coastal marshland. Some of the Audubon sanctuaries protect the most important nesting colonies of such rare species as the roseate spoonbill, the reddish egret, and the wood stork. The extraordinary comeback of the American and snowy egrets, threatened with extinction a few decades ago, has to a large extent been made possible by the protection of their nesting colonies by this society.

National Wildlife Federation, 1412 Sixteenth Street, N.W., Washington, D.C. 20036. Organized in 1936, the National Wildlife Federation is the largest private conservation organization in the world. It is a non-profit association of state organizations and their affiliated local conservation clubs representing more than 2 million people. The federation is proud of the fact that over the past several years no professional fund raisers have been employed and no part of the federation's income goes to any consulting or advertising agency. The federation's prime objective is to encourage through all educational means the intelligent management of the life-sustaining resources of the earth—its soils, its water, its forests and plant life, its wildlife—and to promote and encourage the pursuit of knowledge and a greater appreciation of these resources.

Save-the-Redwoods League, 114 Samson Street, San Francisco, California 94104. The Save-the-Redwoods League's primary program is: To rescue from destruction representative areas of our primeval forests. To cooperate with the California State Park Commission, the National Park Service, and other agencies, in establishing redwood parks and other parks and reservations. To purchase redwood groves by private subscription. To cooperate with the California State Highway Commission and other agencies in assuring the preservation of trees and roadside beauty along highways. To support reforestation and conservation of our forest areas.

Since 1918, the league has raised more than 12 million dollars to purchase outstanding redwood groves. These funds, when matched by the State of California, have purchased more than 102,000 acres now in twenty-eight state redwood parks, of which over 50,000 acres are virgin coast redwoods. These parks would cost an estimated two hundred fifty million dollars if purchased today. The Save-the-Redwood League's primary program includes adding to the major redwood parks at least 50,000 necessary acres of privately owned land, since each park must be an ecologically complete watershed unit so that its beauty and integrity will be preserved.

Sierra Club, 1050 Mills Tower, 220 Bush Street, San Francisco, California 94104. The Sierra Club was founded by John Muir in 1892 to help people explore, enjoy, and protect parks, wilderness, waters, forests, and wildlife, and to rescue places that made America

beautiful. The club is of, by, and for people of all ages; its members, now numbering 35,000, are from all walks of life. The only requirement for membership is that the applicant be twelve years old or older and interested in the purposes that the Sierra Club seeks to serve in the public interest.

The Izaak Walton League of America, 1326 Waukegan Road, Glenview, Illinois 20025. Founded in 1922, the league is a democratically organized group of citizens interested in conservation and outdoor recreation. It has but one policy—that the natural resources of America should be managed and used to provide the greatest benefits of all kinds in the long run. The league looks on conservation as the art and science by which man strives to achieve the best relationship with his natural environment. Conservation is managed human ecology. Thus, the league recognizes that man is above all a biological organism and that every action which he takes inescapably influences all of nature, including man himself. Conservation is the discipline by which man plans and acts with care, under the guidance of knowledge, to preserve nature.

The Wilderness Society, 729 Fifteen Street, N.W., Washington, D.C. 20005. Established in 1935, this society is a national conservation organization dedicated to preserving wilderness—to carry on an educational program concerning the value of wilderness and how it may best be used and preserved in the public interest, to make and encourage scientific studies concerning wilderness, and to mobilize cooperation in resisting the invasion of wilderness. It is the society's belief that the entire nation is losing something of value when a highway is built in a wilderness, when a primeval forest is logged, when airplanes bring the noise of urban life into a wilderness and destroy the charm of remoteness, or when mechanical civilization encroaches in any way on the last remnants of wilderness. The society further believes that wilderness is a valuable natural resource that belongs to the people and that its preservation—for educational, scientific, and recreational use—is part of a balanced conservation program essential in the survival of our civilized culture.

Take an active part in civic matters. Keep yourself informed of everything that goes on in your community of interest to you and your neighborhood, particularly that which concerns planning and zoning. Speak up and vote at town meetings. Write letters to the editor of the local newspaper. Organize a group of people with common interests, and make your opinion known in public. Arrange lectures and instigate educational programs. Invite outside speakers of national repute to talk about conservation and show movies or slides. Work toward creating a community spirit favorable to conservation principles—a spirit that will eventually permeate the schools as well as affect the thinking of businessmen and civic leaders, perhaps induce them to give money for a park, a bird sanctuary, or a wildlife refuge—creating in effect a local "citizen's committee on beautification."

Support local state, and national forest fire prevention programs. Fire is one of the greatest enemies of the forest, second in destructiveness only to insect pests. To minimize potential fire losses, organized fire protection is now provided for 96 per cent of the nation's forest land. Primary in importance are modern road systems which enable fire-fighting crews and equipment to reach the fire quickly. Logging operations are conducted so as to minimize the concentrations of flammable material left on the forest floor. Large standing dead trees ("snags") which attract lightning and may start fires are felled by special crews. Slash burning is a common practice in the West, while in the South the "prescribed burning" conducted periodically by some operators serves to prevent brown spots and eliminate flammable scrub growth from pine forests without hurting the residual stand. Fire lookout towers, water holes, conventional and special fire-fighting equipment, fire-crew facilities, and communication by telephone, radio, and television are maintained throughout the dry season.

The goal of all fire fighting is to extinguish a fire while it is still small. The actual plan for fighting each fire depends on the type of forest and amount of brush, the nearness of roads and water, the weather, and many other factors, but in general the procedure is as follows:

The moment a fire spotter sees a wisp of smoke from his lookout tower or airplane, he reports it to the dispatcher for that area. The dispatcher mobilizes the nearest crew of trained fire fighters. As soon as the men arrive they begin to cut down the trees and brush necessary to make a path several feet wide. The path

is cleared of everything flammable and is scraped down to fresh dirt. A backfire is started from this line which burns from the line toward the main fire. When the flames meet, the fires die for lack of fuel. The fire fighting crew then makes certain that the blaze does not start anew from smoldering embers.

Trucks carrying up to 500 gallons of water each, powerful pumps, bulldozers, and plows are used when roads make it possible to get close to the fire. Two-way radios keep fire bosses in touch with lookouts, other fire crews, and headquarters. Airplanes may help in several ways. Smoke jumpers may parachute to earth to fight fires in isolated areas that cannot be reached by roads. Observers sometimes use airplanes to study the progress of the flames and issue directions to ground crews by radio. A recent development is dropping slurries and chemical foam in the path of the fire to slow it down. The technique calls for airplanes to make runs over the forest fire and drop charges of a mixture of sodium calcium borate and water. Modern firefighting methods have drastically reduced the extent of their damages, but in spite of all efforts at prevention fires break out somewhere in the forest every day. In 1938, for example, a total of 232, 229 fires destroyed 33,815,100 acres of forest land in the United States; but in 1960, only 103,387 forest fires were reported and the burned area was down to 4,478,188 acres. However, 90 per cent of all these fires were caused by man's carelessness or malevolence: of 89,627 fires reported on protected forest areas in 1960, only 11,068 were due to lightning; debris burning started 27,870 fires; deliberate incendiarism 21,162; careless smoking 16,030; the rest were caused (in order of descending numbers) by railroads, campers, loggers, and "miscellaneous agents."

The only practical way to reduce the number of forest fires is through education. Vigorous public campaigns are waged by the U.S. Forest Service and their symbol, Smokey the Bear, is as familiar to the schoolchildren of some faraway rural district as it is to New York's subway straphangers. Everybody has read Smokey the Bear's admonition "Only you can prevent forest fires!" and knows his ABC: "Always hold matches 'til cold! Be sure to drown fires! Crush all smokes dead out!" Much credit for reducing the annual number of forest fires must also be given to the Keep America Green campaign sponsored by American Forest Products Industries,

Inc., an educational program designed to enlist public support for forest-fire prevention. At present, Keep Green organizations have been established in thirty-six states. They distribute educational leaflets, booklets, and pamphlets, place their message on posters and billboards, and make spot announcements over radio and television stations. They are worthy of everyone's support.

Plant a tree. Better still, plant several trees, or urge that trees be planted in your street, your neighborhood, your community. Much of the charm and beauty of an "old-fashioned" New England town—or, for that matter, of Paris—is its majestic old shade trees. On the other hand, many of our "modern" cities are cold and ugly precisely because they have so few trees.

Home owners can increase both the beauty and the value of their property by planting trees. However, before anyone rushes to the tree nursery and buys a tree he should sit down and thoughtfully work out his project in the form of a sketch and a map. Mistakes made on paper are easily and inexpensively corrected, whereas, once a tree is planted, moving it is a costly chore. Here are some of the points that should be considered:

Trees can be planted for shade, wind protection, frame and border, and background. Make sketches of your house from different angles or work from photographs, and draw in the tree or trees as you visualize them when fully grown. Then transfer their positions to a map and plant the trees accordingly.

While you are still working on paper, consider the size to which your future trees will grow. If you visualize your home set in trees forty to fifty feet high at maturity, be careful not to select a species that will grow 100 feet. Consult your tree nurseryman or a landscape architect. Better still, see a mature tree like the one you are thinking of planting. The trunk size and crown spread may surprise you.

Make allowance for possible overhead wires—telephone, light, or power lines—when you are selecting and arranging trees. It is usually more desirable to move (or remove) a tree than to mutilate it so that it does not conflict with overhead wires.

Plant your trees far enough away from buildings, walks, and driveways to enable them to spread and grow naturally and avoid costly moving later. You may be surprised how fast, high, and wide some trees can grow. Do not plant trees where they will eventually block the view. The roots of some trees, especially willows and cottonwoods, will clog sewer pipes if planted too close to a soil line.

The trees you intend to plant must be adapted to the soil and climate of their new location. Some trees, such as silver maple, yellow poplar, and Siberian elm, have brittle branches that break easily in high winds and ice storms. If you live in a location where the latter are likely occurrences it would be better to choose pin oak, white ash, locust, or sycamore — trees that grow erect and tall but are more resistant to breakage.

Some trees have a reputation for being "messy" because they litter the ground more than others with leaves and debris; catalpa, hickory, butternut, and the ashes belong in this group. If you wish to avoid raking leaves in fall, you might consider planting evergreens, which have the further advantage of being green all year round but the disadvantage of offering little or no useful shade in summer.

Certain fast-growing trees are intolerant of shade. Aspen, cottonwood, and some of the poplars like to stand alone. Do not place them in groups. Maples and elms form mats of surface roots. They are greedy feeders, and if you want a green and healthy lawn beneath their shade, you will have to water and fertilize the ground constantly.

Planting a tree requires knowledge and skill. Most people are better off if they leave this operation to a reputable nurseryman, who also usually guarantees the newly planted tree for one year; should it die within this time, he will replace it at his own expense. Do-it-yourselfers must be warned that there is more to tree-planting than merely digging a hole and dumping the tree in. Unless the hole is dug with due regard to width and depth, the soil drained and prepared adequately, the tree planted correctly at the proper time, its branches pruned and its trunk braced as required by the respective species, and proper after care provided in regard to watering and fertilizing, its chances of survival are slim. A modest expenditure for a good gardener's handbook and careful adherence to its instructions are the best guarantees that your tree will live.

Notes on the Photographs

Professional photographers as well as botanists know that tree photography is a much more difficult art than it would seem. I find that making good photographs of trees depends on four basic conditions: first, the tree selected must be typical of its species in growth pattern; second, its surroundings and background must be such that the final picture will be scientifically informative and esthetically pleasing; third, atmospheric and light conditions must be suitable; and, finally, the season must be right—it makes a great deal of difference whether a tree is in sparse foliage in spring, in dense foliage in summer, colorful in fall, or revealing its skeletal structure in winter.

It is a mistake to assume that a characteristic tree will automatically make a characteristic picture. Too often, in the photograph, the tree might be any one of several similar species; or it is obscured by other nearby trees; or it blends with trees growing behind it; or the effect of the picture is marred by the inclusion of buildings, sections of a highway, telephone wires, power lines, or other distracting elements. While I worked on this book, many well-meaning people who were trying to help told me of specific trees they had seen and admired. But invariably, whenever I took the trouble to find the recommended tree, I found that, although it usually was beautiful and typical, it was also totally unphotogenic because of unsuitable surroundings. Since unfavorable conditions can spoil the effect of even the most beautiful tree, I make it a rule never to photograph a tree unless my four conditions for a successful picture are met. As a result, I must have looked at thousands of carefully selected trees before I found the specimens shown in this book.

I took my pictures over a period of many years. Since tree photography is a time-consuming business, to get the best possible results I made it a habit to photograph trees whenever I had the opportunity—on assignments, on vacation, on my travels in Europe. And to round out my collection, during the spring and early summer of 1966 I took one final, twelve-week, 11,000-mile automobile trip devoted exclusively to tree photography, covering the larger part of the United States from the Appalachians to the Everglades and from the Atlantic to the Pacific.

The photographs in this book were chosen from a total of 314 rolls of no. 120 black-and-white and 118 rolls of color film, plus a number of larger color transparencies—some 5,000 shots altogether. I contact-printed all the black-and-white negatives, edited the contact sheets, and made 8 by 10-inch enlargements of some 700 promising-looking shots. These work prints served as the reservoir from which I drew the photographs for the black-and-white reproductions in this book. The color reproductions were made directly from the transparencies.

All black-and-white photographs were made on Kodak Tri-X Pan Film rated at 360 ASA and developed in D-76. All color photographs were made on Kodak Ektachrome Daylight Film rated at ASA 64. Most of the shots were made with the camera mounted on a tripod. For readers who are interested in photo-technical data, the following list tells how each picture was made.

Page	Camera	Lens	Exposure
1	Linhof 5×7″	210 mm	$1/25$ at f/22
2	Rolleiflex	75 mm	$1/100$ at f/22
3	Mamiyaflex	18 cm	$1/50$ at f/8
4	Rolleiflex	75 mm	$1/100$ at f/20
5	Rolleiflex	80 mm	$1/100$ at f/16
6	Mamiyaflex	135 mm	$1/100$ at f/14
7	Rolleiflex	80 mm	$1/100$ at f/20
8/9	Peko view 2¼×3¼″	135 mm	$1/25$ at f/22
10	Rolleiflex	75 mm	$1/50$ at f/16
11	Rolleiflex	80 mm	$1/100$ at f/8
12	Rolleiflex	75 mm	$1/100$ at f/22, y. f.
13	Rolleiflex	75 mm	$1/50$ at f/22, r. f.
14	Linhof 5×7″	120 mm	$1/2$ at f/20
15	Rolleiflex	75 mm	$1/100$ at f/16
16	Rolleiflex	80 mm	1 sec. at f/12
17	Rolleiflex	80 mm	$1/100$ at f/16
18	Rolleiflex	75 mm	$1/100$ at f/22
19	Rolleiflex	75 mm	$1/50$ at f/16
20	Rolleiflex	80 mm	$1/100$ at f/22
21	Rolleiflex	80 mm	$1/100$ at f/22
22	Rolleiflex	80 mm	$1/100$ at f/22
23	Rolleiflex	80 mm	$1/50$ at f/16
24	Rolleiflex	75 mm	$1/25$ at f/16, r. f.
25	Rolleiflex	75 mm	$1/100$ at f/20
26	Rolleiflex	80 mm	$1/100$ at f/22
27	Rolleiflex	80 mm	$1/100$ at f/22
28	Rolleiflex	75 mm	$1/100$ at f/22
29	Rolleiflex	80 mm	$1/100$ at f/22
30	Rolleiflex	75 mm	$1/100$ at f/20
31	Rolleiflex	80 mm	$1/100$ at f/22
32	Rolleiflex	80 mm	$1/100$ at f/22
33	Peko view 2¼×3¼″	21 cm	$1/25$ at f/22
34/35	Peko view 2¼×3¼″	135 mm	$1/25$ at f/22
36	Peko view 2¼×3¼″	21 cm	$1/25$ at f/22
37	Rolleiflex	80 mm	$1/100$ at f/16
38	Mamiyaflex	135 mm	$1/100$ at f/16
39	Rolleiflex	80 mm	$1/25$ at f/20
40	Rolleiflex	80 mm	$1/50$ at f/16, r. f.
41	Rolleiflex	80 mm	$1/100$ at f/20
42	Mamiyaflex	180 mm	$1/100$ at f/22
43	Rolleiflex	75 mm	$1/100$ at f/16
44	Rolleiflex	80 mm	$1/50$ at f/16, r. f.
45	Rolleiflex	80 mm	$1/100$ at f/22
46	Rolleiflex	75 mm	$1/50$ at f/22
47	Rolleiflex	80 mm	$1/100$ at f/22
48	Rolleiflex	75 mm	$1/100$ at f/22
49	Mamiyaflex	80 mm	$1/50$ at f/16, y. f.
50	Rolleiflex	180 mm	$1/100$ at f/22
51	Rolleiflex	80 mm	$1/25$ at f/22
52	Rolleiflex	80 mm	$1/100$ at f/14
53	Mamiyaflex	135 mm	$1/5$ at f/12
54/55	Peko view 2¼×3¼″	135 mm	$1/2$ at f/16
56	Peko view 2¼×3¼″	21 cm	$1/2$ at f/16
57	Mamiyaflex	180 mm	$1/8$ at f/25
58	Rolleiflex	80 mm	$1/50$ at f/16
59	Rolleiflex	80 mm	$1/10$ at f/22

Page	Camera	Lens	Exposure
60	Rolleiflex	80 mm	$1/10$ at f/16
61	Rolleiflex	80 mm	$1/100$ at f/16
62	Rolleiflex	80 mm	$1/100$ at f/16
63	Rolleiflex	80 mm	$1/100$ at f/16
64	Rolleiflex	80 mm	$1/100$ at f/20
65	Rolleiflex	80 mm	$1/100$ at f/16
66	Rolleiflex	80 mm	$1/100$ at f/16
67	Rolleiflex	80 mm	$1/100$ at f/16
68	Rolleiflex	80 mm	$1/100$ at f/16
69	Rolleiflex	75 mm	$1/100$ at f/22
70	Rolleiflex	80 mm	$1/25$ at f/16
71	Rolleiflex	80 mm	$1/25$ at f/14
72	Rolleiflex	80 mm	$1/100$ at f/16
73	Rolleiflex	80 mm	$1/100$ at f/20
74	Rolleiflex	80 mm	$1/100$ at f/20
75	Rolleiflex	75 mm	$1/100$ at f/20
76	Rolleiflex	75 mm	$1/10$ at f/22
77	Peko view $2\frac{1}{4} \times 3\frac{1}{4}''$	135 mm	$1/25$ at f/22
78	Mamiyaflex	135 mm	$1/2$ at f/14
79	Mamiyaflex	135 mm	$1/2$ at f/16
80	Mamiyaflex	80 mm	$1/2$ at f/16
81	Rolleiflex	80 mm	$1/100$ at f/22
82	Rolleiflex	80 mm	$1/100$ at f/20
83	Rolleiflex	80 mm	$1/100$ at f/16
84	Rolleiflex	80 mm	$1/100$ at f/20
85	Rolleiflex	80 mm	$1/100$ at f/16
86	Rolleiflex	80 mm	$1/100$ at f/22
87	Rolleiflex	80 mm	$1/100$ at f/22
88	Rolleiflex	80 mm	$1/100$ at f/16
89	Rolleiflex	75 mm	$1/100$ at f/20
90	Rolleiflex	80 mm	$1/100$ at f/16
91	Rolleiflex	75 mm	$1/100$ at f/16, y. f.
92	Mamiyaflex	80 mm	$1/50$ at f/16
93	Mamiyaflex	80 mm	$1/100$ at f/16
94	Rolleiflex	80 mm	$1/50$ at f/16
95	Rolleiflex	80 mm	$1/100$ at f/16
96	Rolleiflex	80 mm	$1/50$ at f/16
97	Peko view $2\frac{1}{4} \times 3\frac{1}{4}''$	160 mm	1 sec. at f/16
98–99	Peko view $2\frac{1}{4} \times 3\frac{1}{4}''$	240 mm	1 sec. at f/16
100	Mamiyaflex	180 mm	$1/2$ at f/16
101	Rolleiflex	80 mm	$1/10$ at f/16
102	Rolleiflex	75 mm	$1/5$ at f/22
103	Rolleiflex	80 mm	$1/100$ at f/20
104	Rolleiflex	80 mm	$1/100$ at f/22
105	Rolleiflex	80 mm	$1/100$ at f/22
106	Rolleiflex	75 mm	$1/100$ at f/22
107	Rolleiflex	75 mm	$1/100$ at f/16
108	Rolleiflex	80 mm	$1/25$ at f/22
109	Rolleiflex	80 mm	$1/25$ at f/22
110	Rolleiflex	80 mm	$1/25$ at f/16
111	Rolleiflex	80 mm	$1/100$ at f/20
112	Rolleiflex	80 mm	$1/100$ at f/22
113	Rolleiflex	80 mm	$1/100$ at f/22
114	Rolleiflex	80 mm	$1/100$ at f/20
115	Rolleiflex	80 mm	$1/100$ at f/22
116	Rolleiflex	80 mm	$1/100$ at f/16
117	Linhof $5 \times 7''$	210 mm	$1/50$ at f/20
118–119	Linhof $5 \times 7''$	210 mm	$1/25$ at f/16
120–121	Linhof $5 \times 7''$	320 mm	$1/25$ at f/18
122–123	Linhof $5 \times 7''$	210 mm	$1/10$ at f/18
124	Peko view $2\frac{1}{4} \times 3\frac{1}{4}''$	90 mm	$1/5$ at f/18
125	Peko view $2\frac{1}{4} \times 3\frac{1}{4}''$	135 mm	$1/10$ at f/22
126	Rolleiflex	80 mm	$1/100$ at f/20
127	Peko view $2\frac{1}{4} \times 3\frac{1}{4}''$	135 mm	$1/25$ at f/22
128	Linhof $4 \times 5''$	75 mm	$1/5$ at f/16
129	Linhof $4 \times 5''$	75 mm	$1/5$ at f/16
130	Linhof $4 \times 5''$	135 mm	$1/10$ at f/16
131	Linhof $4 \times 5''$	135 mm	$1/10$ at f/16
132	Rolleiflex	80 mm	$1/100$ at f/16
133	Rolleiflex	80 mm	$1/50$ at f/16
134	Rolleiflex	80 mm	$1/25$ at f/22
135	Rolleiflex	80 mm	$1/25$ at f/22
136	Rolleiflex	75 mm	$1/100$ at f/22
137	Rolleiflex	75 mm	$1/100$ at f/22
138	Rolleiflex	75 mm	$1/50$ at f/16, r. f.
139	Rolleiflex	75 mm	$1/100$ at f/16
140	Rolleiflex	75 mm	$1/25$ at f/16, r. f.
141	Rolleiflex	80 mm	$1/25$ at f/11
142–143	Linhof $5 \times 7''$	210 mm	$1/10$ at f/25
144	Linhof $5 \times 7''$	210 mm	$1/10$ at f/18
145	Rolleiflex	80 mm	$1/100$ at f/22
146	Rolleiflex	80 mm	$1/100$ at f/16
147	Rolleiflex	80 mm	$1/100$ at f/16
148	Rolleiflex	80 mm	$1/100$ at f/11
149	Rolleiflex	80 mm	$1/100$ at f/16
150	Rolleiflex	80 mm	$1/50$ at f/22
151	Rolleiflex	80 mm	$1/25$ at f/22
152	Rolleiflex	80 mm	$1/50$ at f/22
153	Rolleiflex	80 mm	$1/50$ at f/22
154	Rolleiflex	80 mm	$1/50$ at f/22
155	Rolleiflex	80 mm	$1/100$ at f/16
156	Rolleiflex	80 mm	$1/50$ at f/22
157	Rolleiflex	80 mm	$1/50$ at f/16
158	Rolleiflex	80 mm	$1/50$ at f/16
159	Rolleiflex	80 mm	$1/25$ at f/22
160	Rolleiflex	80 mm	$1/100$ at f/22

NOTE: I very rarely use filters. Whenever this was the case, it is indicated in the above list: y. f. means a yellow filter with a factor of 2; r. f. means a red filter with a factor of 5. Since, as a rule, trees are subjects of more than average contrast, to avoid excessively contrasty negatives, I always exposed my black-and-white films generously and developed them in a somewhat shorter time than normal. As a result, virtually all my negatives printed well on no. 2 paper.

INDEX

(Page numbers in parenthesis refer to picture pages)

flagellate, 58
flitch, 18
floods, 22
flower, 53–54; imperfect, 54; parts of, 53; perfect, 53, 54; pistillate, 54; staminate, 54
flowering dogwood, 67, 79 (71)
food chain, 89
food for trees, 57
forest, 89–96; commercial, 15, 105; Boreal, 93; Central Hardwood, 94; hemlock-hardwood, 94, 102 (142–43); Northern, 94; northern hardwood, 39; Pacific Coast, 94; privately owned, 105; Rocky Mountain, 94; Southern, 96; tropical, 96; United States, 105; virgin, 25
forest fires, 91, 108
forest products industries, 10
fossil plants, 37
Founders' Grove, 69
Founders' Tree, 69
Fourdrinier, 20
fruit, 54–55; accessory, 55; edible tree, 21; multiple, 55, simple, 55
fuelwood, 21
fungus diseases, 92

Gamete, 53
General Grant Tree, 34, 81
General Sherman Tree, 34, 81
genes, 51
geotropism, 59
ginkgo, 30, 35, 38, 41, 46, 60, 76, 79 (30, 37)
girdling, 66
glucose, 74
Gnetales, 38, 39
grana, 74
Grand Canyon, 27
grape sugar, 74
gray birch, 67, 86 (64)
groundwater, 23
growth, *see* annual growth rings, tree growth
guard cells, 73
gullying, 25
gum, 21
Gymnosperms, 38, 39, 54
gypsy moth, 91

Hainbuche, 103 (148)
hand, development of, 29
hardwood, 97
Hart Tree, 34
harvest cut, 17
heartwood, 56, 66
Helmont, J.B. van, 51
hemlock, 86
herbaceous plants, 33
herbs, 33
Hercules' club, 77, 80 (90)
hickory, 77, 86, 97
honey locust, 54
hop hornbeam, 67 (70)
horse-chestnut, 41, 44, 46, 54, 76 (22, 23)
horsetails, 38
Humboldt Redwoods State Park, 22, 34, 69

Identification of trees, 42
imbibition, 57
insect pests, 90–91
integrated sawmill, 18
ironwood, 97
Isle Royal National Park, 90
Izaak Walton League, 107

Jack pine, 91
Jordan, 20
juniper, 97

Kaibab deer, 90
Kaibab Forest, 90
kapok, 88 (114)
Kentucky coffee tree, 54, 77
knees, cypress, 87

Laboratory for Tree-Ring Research, 47, 98
Land Ordinance of 1785, 12
leaf mosaic, 59
leaves, 53, 73; arrangement of (paired, spiral, whorled), 76; compound, 77; doubly compound, 77; lobed, 77; mitten-shaped, 77; needle-like, 76; palmately compound, 77; palmately lobed, 75; pinnately compound, 77; pinnately lobed, 75; shapes of, 78; simple, 77
legume, 54
Lepidodendron, 38

lignin, 33, 56
live oaks, 28, 41, 44, 63–64 (52–56)
loam, 26
logging, salvage, 17
Lombardy poplar, 104 (157)
London plane tree, 42, 103 (149)
long-leaf pine, 60–61 (42)
lumber consumption, 15, 17
lumber industry, American, 15
lumbering, 15, 16
lumberjack, 11
Lyell, Charles, 25

Madroña, 67 (60)
magnolia, 44
mahogany, 65, 96
maidenhair tree, 60 (37)
Malthus, Thomas, 27
man, origin of, 29
mangrove, 87, 96 (104, 105, 124)
maple, 76, 97, 101
McKinley Tree, 34
Meganeura, 38
mesophyll, 73
Metasequoia, 81–82
Middleton Gardens, 64
midrib, 77
Midsummer Day, 31
mitosis, 52
Monocotyledons, 38
Montezuma cypress, 34
mulberry, 41, 55, 77, 78 (82)
myths, 29

Names of trees, 35–36
National Audubon Society, 106
National Wildlife Federation, 106
New York Times, The, 10
nucleus, 51
nut, 54
nutrients, plant, 26

Oak, 31, 44, 63, 76, 86, 97, 98 (17, 48, 49, 128, 158, 159)
Osage orange, 55
osmosis, 57
ovary, 53, 54
oxygen, 74, 75